ENDORSEMENT

Connie and Wade Urban's unique approach to ministry is a blessing to the Body of Christ. Their obedience to God and their love for the Body of Christ is refreshing to see. I have seen deliverance and healing through their ministry. Therefore, I would, without a doubt, highly recommend their books and teaching materials to an individual and also to a church organization.

Richard Ware
Founder and Senior Pastor
Higher Praise Worship Center
Connersville, Indiana

YOUR HOLY SPIRIT ARSENAL

YOUR HOLY SPIRIT ARSENAL

Waging Victorious Warfare
Through the Gifts of the Spirit

Wade and Connie Hunter-Urban

DESTINY IMAGE® PUBLISHERS, INC.
P.O. Box 310, Shippensburg, PA 17257-0310
"Promoting Inspired Lives."

Previously published as *Our Holy Spirit Arsenal* by Tate Publishing
Previous ISBN: 978-1-63367-470-7

This book and all other Destiny Image and Destiny Image Fiction books are available at Christian bookstores and distributors worldwide.

Cover design by Eileen Rockwell

For more information on foreign distributors, call 717-532-3040.
Reach us on the Internet: www.destinyimage.com.

ISBN 13 TP: 978-0-7684-1895-8
ISBN 13 eBook: 978-0-7684-1896-5
ISBN 13 HC: 978-0-7684-1898-9
ISBN 13 LP: 978-0-7684-1897-2

For Worldwide Distribution, Printed in the U.S.A.
1 2 3 4 5 6 7 8 / 22 21 20 19 18

ACKNOWLEDGMENTS

W̲e would like to thank the following people who have helped us realize our calling of teaching others about growing in their gifts of Holy Spirit:

- Our lovely Lord who has demonstrated Himself to us many times.
- Our friends who supported us as we received the revelation to teach Bible study then workshops about Holy Spirit.
- Each other for truly being helpmates on this journey of growth and of teaching others about the wonders of Holy Spirit.
- Our parents who are with Jesus—Ernest and Audrey Sampson-Hunter and Gordon Urban—and our mother, Joan Urban, who all started us on our Holy Spirit walks and helped nurture that passion within us.
- Our daughters—Lissa, Kristin, Rachel, Jennifer, and Jillian—who enriched our lives the moment God allowed us to be their parents. Parenting has demonstrated much about our own relationships with the Father.
- Our siblings—Beth, Verne, Suzy, Lynda, Phillip, Becky, Liz, Anita, and Jason—who are all a blessing and inspiration to us.

A special thanks to Wade's friend and business partner Scott, with whom he has traveled on many business highs and lows, but through those times has learned dependence on Holy Spirit.

CONTENTS

FOREWORD

The devil hates revelation knowledge because it leads to deliverance. When people discover the truth about God's power, they are set free, but when they lack this spiritual knowledge they are held captive in their ignorance. God told Isaiah, "Therefore my people have gone into captivity, because they have no knowledge" (Isa. 5:13). Spiritual knowledge is power!

Wade and Connie will lead you through the Word of God, connecting you to Jesus, the only right source of power. I have watched them operate in God's supernatural power as they make themselves available to God. We have been privileged to have them as guest speakers/teachers of God's Word at Positive Impact on several occasions. Each time, they have enlightened us with the revelation of God's Word through the Holy Spirit. God designed you to dwell in His presence, understand His heart, and experience His divine power—transforming your life and enabling you to do miracles and wonders that reveal His majesty on earth.

Through insights about the Holy Spirit in *Your Holy Spirit Arsenal*, Wade and Connie will help you personally develop a passion and thirst for God and be ignited by God's fire to do the impossible—becoming a dynamic witness, seeing lives transformed, and being changed forever. Connie and I have been friends since childhood, and I am honored to have her and Wade in my life now. I have watched them as they have carried God's Word and led His people into deeper relationship with the Holy Spirit.

1

Jesus will come for a glorious church that will manifest God's tangible and visible glory with miracles, healings, signs, and wonders. Every believer who is sanctified and separated for Him will be a vessel of both the latter and former glories that will invade this world. I believe the day is here when a carrier of God's glory full of the Holy Spirit will step through the door of a hospital, and all patients will be instantly healed. The earth is full of God's glory, and He is revealing it to this generation in order to bring great manifestations. God is raising a generation with a different mentality—a generation willing to run and be carriers of His divine glory. We must decide today whether or not we want to enter into the realm of His glory through the anointing of the Holy Spirit. It is a blessing to be alive and to witness God's glory manifested everywhere, right in front of our eyes!

Wade and Connie's ministry goal is to encourage believers to go from merely having information about the Holy Spirit to experiencing Him. As you read *Your Holy Spirit Arsenal,* your spiritual life will develop. Faith is strongest when we have the greatest knowledge from God through the Holy Spirit. I encourage you to take these steps to walk in the Spirit and experience a change of mindset for more aspects of the Holy Spirit. "For there are three that bear witness in heaven: the Father, the Word, and the Holy Spirit; and these three are one" (1 John 5:7). Enjoy your journey through *Your Holy Spirit Arsenal* as God gives you revelation knowledge of His power!

Kara'lynne V. Brubaker
Founder and Co-pastor of Positive Impact Ministries, Inc.
Saint Petersburg, Florida

PREFACE

Connie

When my twin daughters were babies, they decided early who would be Mommy's or Daddy's girl. Jennifer had bonded with me during an early hospital stay; so whatever we did as a family, she always had to be with Mommy. When we all lay down, she wanted to lie by me. If we walked, she held my hand. If circumstances required her to be by Daddy, she cried until she could get beside me. That left Jillian rarely able to hang out with Mommy.

One night as we watched TV, Jennifer was on the loveseat with her dad while Jill stretched out beside me, head on my lap and arm raised for me to scratch. We didn't enjoy that scenario for long, though, before Jennifer once again threw a fit because she was "stuck" beside Daddy. The longer we sat, the more she protested.

"Why don't you sit by me tonight?" her dad said, his low voice cajoling her. She shook her head and cried louder.

"I want Mommy."

"But I love it when you sit by me."

"I want Mommeee."

"Don't you like me, Jennifer?"

"I like Mommy. I want Mommy. Mommeee!" As she reached my way, her pleading eyes locked on mine and big tears tugged at my heart, as they still do after all these years.

3

Ever the peacemaker, Jill sat up, then stood up slowly. "Otay, Jiffer. I sit by Daddy." Dropping her head in defeat, she shuffled a couple steps across the brown carpet toward her dad, her small lips puckering, mouth turning downward, and head shifting slightly from side to side. Jennifer immediately stopped crying and jumped up to trade places.

"No!" I said firmly. "Just because you want something doesn't mean you always get your way, Jennifer." I looked at her. "You stay with Daddy. Mommy has two babies." Amid Jennifer's wails when she knew her plans were thwarted, Jill jumped back on the couch by me.

"Jiffer, Mommy say ah don hat to!"

The matter was settled. That night in very ineloquent language, Jill clearly made her point. In years to come, her communication skills would constantly improve. "Jiffer" would become "Jennifer," "ah don" would become "I don't," and "hat to" would turn into "have to." She would later understand grammatical usage should be "Mommy says" not "Mommy say." She would listen, observe, learn, and internalize; but for that night in our Brookville, Indiana home, her words were just fine. Her sister, dad, and I understood perfectly.

In my time as an English teacher, I realized that one's ability to use language well generally reflects experiences. Most grammatically articulate students were those brought up by educated parents with great grammar. In contrast, despite intelligence, many students reared in homes where less-than-pristine English was used still struggled in high school. Overcoming this hurdle wasn't impossible, but their usage wasn't as natural as those whose backgrounds made them internalize good English basics.

Mastering a language is similar to operating in Holy Spirit. You learn how to use the gifts in two ways—experience and education. Even biblical saints learned these ways. Though Elijah taught many at his schools for the prophets, Elisha learned by doing in his training season with his mentor, Elijah. I'm sure he refined his gifts, which ultimately brought a double portion while they travelled dusty roads just doing Holy Spirit's work. However, although advantages exist to learning by doing in this Holy Spirit walk, you need both to become a consummate operator in the gifts. No matter where you are right now, if you continue to use your gifts, just like Jill you'll get better. For right now, though, you're fine where you are. You don't expect children to be born having mastered the language or anything else. By the same token, God doesn't expect a beginner to be perfect in his/her operation of the gifts—it's a process.

I began employing Holy Spirit's gifts before I was a teenager, so because of my background I'm sensitive to the Spirit. However, when I was growing up, our church operated prolifically in the gifts but offered little teaching. Then I married Wade. He knew about the gifts also, but he'd been brought up in a church that didn't operate in them. His exposure basically came through reading everything he could find and seeing the gifts operate on a limited scale. As a result, he knew cognitively how they worked but had little personal experience. Over the years since we've married, we've both grown because we learned from each other's strengths.

You're also probably in one camp or the other with varying exposures, familiarity, and phases of your Holy Spirit walk. You'll grow as you read our instructions and experiences, but truly maturing will come when you jump in and do it. You can read, talk to others, and hear stories, but practical application is crucial. If you affiliate with believers who allow the gifts to operate in their midst, you can learn from actually using the gifts, making mistakes, and letting others mentor you.

The best Teacher, though, is Holy Spirit Himself. He accomplishes our unceasing progression by guiding us through each experience. Learning to operate in His gifts is like when Hosea said God "taught Ephraim to walk, taking them by their arms; but they did not know that [God] healed them" (Hos. 11:3). That Scripture speaks to me. We're works in progress, just babes learning to maneuver in our Christian walk. Then along comes our Holy Spirit infilling with His gifts like healing, and we feel amazed and insecure as we make our way in that new, glorious journey. As He takes us by our arms, He directs us like a daddy guides his baby who's learning to walk.

This scenario describes my friend Marci. I had met her a couple times at church, but I wasn't sure who Marci was when a friend said she was going with us on an overnight trip. The morning we were to leave, I spotted her at church, curls piled on her head and her long jacket swaying in rhythm to each step she gingerly bore on her cane. She was heading toward me with a purposeful expression.

"I'm going!" she blurted. "I thought I wasn't, but I know I need to." We chatted a minute, then, after church, started on the five-hour Chicago trip filled with incessant chatter from us three women. Marci and I were still talking the next morning at breakfast when conversation turned to a family member's illness. When I asked if she'd prayed for healing, she cocked her head and put her hand on her face in bewilderment.

"I thought that was too big for God to heal." Then my preacher side kicked in. I talked of God's miracles way bigger than her need—creation, the sun standing still, eyeballs made from mud. As she listened, I knew why Marci had felt the need to come. God wanted to reveal Himself as a reality—a bigger God than she'd known in her years of religion but not relationship with Him.

That's why when she hobbled to my ministry line a few Sunday mornings later, I wasn't surprised. She dared to come for something big—a healing for her knee. She sat on a chair while I perched on the floor and held her foot on my lap. I put my hands around her knee and prayed. Then I allowed Holy Spirit to do His work through the healing gift in my hands. When the prayer was done, Marci, eyes wide with wonder, said she'd felt a current enter her knee and travel up and down her leg. She sat a few minutes, basking in Holy Spirit's power. As she walked away, still relying on that cane, she had discomfort but knew something was different. She decided she'd proceed as if it were healed though she didn't yet see evidence. Marci was Ephraim learning to walk, both physically and spiritually, as she took those faith steps. And God was healing her in the process. That day, she was amazed at how well she traversed her stairs, a task that had limited her to one well-planned trip up and down per day. Then the next weekend, she came to church walking without her cane. Grinning broadly, she excitedly told me about the stairs and how she'd used a regular cart instead of a riding one at the grocery.

A couple months later, her smooth gait was nearly as fast as mine. When I commented, she smiled and grabbed my hand, her bracelets jangling. "I walk anywhere now. And, oh, I've lost nineteen pounds." God never intended anything to stay dormant—not water, not a baby, not believers in their Christian walks, not a woman with a banged-up knee, not operators in Holy Spirit. He wants us to grow—physically, mentally, and spiritually. We're Ephraims, taking the hand of our Father as we learn to walk in the gifts, an exciting step-by-step adventure. Like Marci, we're learning to move in this exciting faith realm where anything's possible. When we hold Holy Spirit's hand, we may stumble at times; but He sets us upright and gives confidence as we grow with each tentative, wondrous step until we become the warriors we were created to be.

This book is written to instruct all us Ephraims who are learning—those who want to know more about the gifts, who are just beginning to operate, and who operate but desire more basics. How the gifts work for us may not be how they work for you; and, as we'll say often, you'll learn more about your own gifts as you use them (see 1 Cor. 12:5). We've tried to describe your tools and weapons and clarify those gifts by explaining specific applications given in your Holy Spirit package. Those are sitting on your spiritual workbench or in your trench, ready to employ when you need them. As this empowerment settles into your spirit, you'll find life in Holy Spirit so much a part of you that you can't imagine having ever lived without Him. That's how it is for me—His gifts are a daily, integral aspect of who I am.

Though Wade and I have different writing styles and experiences, we have a common goal—to help you learn about the precious Holy Spirit. We're scratching the surface of a topic that gets bigger the more we learn about it. I'm thrilled to have you discover more about this wondrous Person whom God has given as our Partner. Allow Him to be your Teacher and Trainer and become real and powerful in your life.

Connie Hunter-Urban

INTRODUCTION

Wade

I am a graduate of the United States Military Academy at West Point and a Vietnam combat veteran. As a minister, my military background provides a unique perspective on many similarities between natural and spiritual warfare. Spiritual basic training educates warriors in everything from fundamentals and use of their weapons of warfare (Holy Spirit's gifts) to advanced individual training, where ministry specialization occurs. These are words of knowledge, wisdom, and discernment of spirits through divine revelation of the enemy's plans, operations, and disposition. Our gifts provide the "shock and awe" air war of intercession to cut off and create confusion in the enemy's camp. The armored tank breakthrough anointing of prophetic action and power gifts bind the enemy and loose his hold on lives. Close-in artillery support of prayer in Holy Spirit covers our infantry attack, engaging and destroying the enemy with power evangelism and deliverance ministries. This coordinated advance secures the objective by teaching and discipleship. Actual spiritual combat destroys the devil's works (see 1 John 3:18).

Believers must be taught how to employ spiritual weapons on life's battlefield. Too often, they're untrained and ill-equipped for spiritual conflicts, so they fail to live triumphantly over satan's tactics. Our earthly mission is to enforce the victory accomplished through the finished work of Lord Jesus Christ. Securing His victory requires training and experience in spiritual warfare and use of spiritual weapons so few have today! Sadly, many have no idea of Holy Spirit's purpose other than vaguely knowing He's a part of the Trinity. Paul admonished the church at Thessalonica: "Do not quench the Spirit" (see 1 Thess. 5:19). *Quenching* means to extinguish or often abolish something. Sounds like the enemy's tactics, doesn't it? (See John 10:10.)

Much of the church today remains unarmed and untrained for spiritual battles because of lack of knowledge (see Hos. 4:6), and they become a casualty of spiritual warfare. Where do we start explaining Holy Spirit so He becomes a practical reality in believers' lives? How do we convince the church that Jesus' earthly ministry in Holy Spirit's power is our example of what *normal* Christianity should look like—healings, miracles, signs, and wonders that displace the enemy from his dominion over men's souls? How do we demonstrate that life devoid of Holy Spirit's gifts and power is *abnormal*, and we haven't been called to be spiritual pacifists but warriors?

Holy Spirit Arsenal: Gifts of Holy Spirit (1 Corinthians 12:4-11)

Holy Spirit's arsenal is comprised of nine weapons—the gifts (*charismas*). When teaching the gifts, it's helpful to divide them into three categories—revelation, speaking, and power. Revelation gifts include words of knowledge, words of wisdom, and discernment of spirits; speaking gifts consist of tongues, interpretation of tongues, and prophecy; power gifts include faith, gifts of healings, and working of miracles. These divisions are for teaching and clarification purposes because Holy Spirit's gifts rarely operate singularly but in cooperation with each other. For example, revelation gifts often precede speaking and power gifts. We'll go into greater detail in later chapters as we discuss operation of these gifts.

All nine gifts of Holy Spirit are yours. The gift of God is Holy Spirit; when you received Jesus as Lord, Holy Spirit came with your complete package of His ability (gifts) and character (fruit). You may have activated His full ability or function in only a few areas, but they're all available. Though you have a well-beaten pathway to a favorite spot in your flower garden, that doesn't mean you can't access the rest of the garden. All Holy Spirit's arsenal is yours for the asking (see Luke 11:9-13).

New Covenant: Centered in Holy Spirit

Jesus said He's the Door as well as the Way, Truth, and Life (see John 10:7-9; 14:6). In effect, Jesus is the Doorway into New Covenant life in Holy Spirit. One aspect of His earthly mission was to preach, teach, and demonstrate the Gospel of the kingdom—life in Holy Spirit. Paul explained, "For the kingdom of God is not eating and drinking, but righteousness and peace and joy in the Holy Spirit" (Rom. 14:17). In other words, the Kingdom is the operation of Holy Spirit in and through believers. Jesus' parables were often about Holy Spirit as He explained the Kingdom of heaven (see Matt. 13 and others). For example:

> *Now when He was asked by the Pharisees when the kingdom of God would come, He answered them and said, "The kingdom of God does not come with observation; nor will they say, 'See here!' or 'See there!'" For indeed, the kingdom of God is within you* (Luke 17:20-21).

Also, in His self-ordination ceremony, Jesus read from Isaiah concerning the anointing:

> *The Spirit of the Lord is upon Me, because He has anointed Me to preach the gospel to the poor; He has sent Me to heal the brokenhearted, to proclaim liberty to the captives and recovery of sight to the blind, to set at liberty those who are oppressed; to proclaim the acceptable year of the Lord* (Luke 4:18-19).

For Jesus, as well as us, the anointing is God's power to destroy satan's works, reverse sin's curse, and demonstrate God's love in tangible ways of restoration, healings, miracle provision, signs, and wonders. That's Holy Spirit. Today, most believers are dwelling in the transitional period of the Gospels, concentrating on the Doorway (Jesus Christ). *Yes, yes,* and *yes!* Jesus is the only Way to the Father; no other way exists. The unconverted desperately need Jesus; however, those already in the Kingdom should advance, grow up in Him, and step through the Doorway into Kingdom reality of Holy Spirit. After all, that was Jesus' emphasis—to prepare His disciples for His physical departure and the coming of the Kingdom in the Person of Holy Spirit.

Let me put it this way. How many realtors attempting to sell a house would take potential buyers to the front door and spend their time admiring the door's paneling, color, and ease of operation, then ask prospects to buy the house? That's exactly what goes on in much of the church today! Why not take buyers into the house through the Doorway and demonstrate Holy Spirit's power by getting them healed, delivered, and freed from sin's bondage? Buying the front door and a future home in heaven when they die is just part of that home. Why not allow them to "taste and see that the Lord is good" (Ps. 34:8) right now? They'll not only want the front door but also the whole house—a permanent *dwelling place* in the Spirit of God (see Eph. 2:22).

If you want Kingdom results, you must employ Kingdom power. This means stepping into the "new thing" God's already prepared and letting go of the old (see Isa. 42:9, 43:18-19). He's looking for those who'll trust Him with all their heart, mind, and body. He's scanning the earth to find your raised hand waving to Him, saying, "Here I am—use me" (see 2 Chron. 16:9, Isa. 6:1-4). God's looking for volunteers to be His warriors!

Our Goal

This book is designed to be a practical guide for deeper Holy Spirit experience, victorious living through His power. As she said in the Preface, Connie's knowledge came from practical application of the gifts while I gained book knowledge, doctrine, and experience in Holy Spirit's operation. This book imparts our understanding from both backgrounds. We're far from being experts! Part of our ministry is to offer a safe place for believers to experience new dimensions of life in Holy Spirit. Ours is a Blacksmith Ministry (see 1 Sam. 13:19-22). An Old Covenant story tells about that. When Saul was king, the Philistines threatened to overtake Israel. Only Saul and his son, Jonathan, had weapons because the Philistines had all the blacksmiths. The Israelites had to go to their enemy to sharpen tools. This strategy kept the Israelites without weapons that could be used against the Philistines.

Our Blacksmith Ministry assists believers in discovering their Holy Spirit gifts (weapons) and provides a platform for them to sharpen their weapons of warfare and tools of harvest. We encourage believers to discover and use their gifts. We also offer in-depth, interactive workshops on aspects of life in Holy Spirit. We publish newsletters and blogs offering insight into Holy Spirit's proceeding word (see Matt. 4:4). Our ministry goal isn't just to provide information but to encourage believers to go from information to expanded experience in Him. We've discovered that experience leads to knowledge and knowledge to understanding. When a person truly understands, Kingdom manifestations occur on purpose! From a deeper understanding of Holy Spirit, Habakkuk 2:14 becomes reality: "For the earth will be filled with the knowledge of the glory of the Lord, as the waters cover the sea." The proliferation of the "knowledge of the glory of the Lord" occurs as believers understand God's ways and purposes through them.

One objective for this book is to provide initiative to step out of the enemy's trap of being a victim to becoming conquerors (see Rom. 8:37). A victorious mindset comes through understanding that in partnership with the Spirit, we're equipped to be resources of Kingdom supply and warriors exercising victory over the enemy. From a victor's perspective, we're qualified for the knowledge of the Lord's glory to be manifested through us to cover the earth. We have God's

Word on that! Paul wrote, "But we all, with unveiled face, beholding as in a mirror the glory of the Lord, are being transformed into the same image from glory to glory, just as by the Spirit of the Lord" (2 Cor. 3:18). Our hope is for the transformation process "from glory to glory" to be accelerated with new levels of glory revealed in and through readers.

Are you prepared to grow to a new level in Christ? Ready, set, let's go deeper in Him!

ONE TO GROW ON: BODY MINISTRY

Connie

Wade and I attend Higher Praise in Connersville, Indiana, where Pastor Richard Ware makes his sermons' points through analogies to life. His simple yet profound comparisons make his sermons come alive and become easily understood. Whether a parody of a commercial or his family's responses to events, he makes that example from daily life fit into a spiritual principle and thus we comprehend his point. In this same manner, by understanding the human body's functioning, we can see how Holy Spirit functions too.

The Church Body

People often call their church family their body because everyone works for common goals (see Eph. 5:23). When someone in our church body loses a loved one, we grieve with him/her and provide a bereavement meal. When someone's in the hospital, we visit and then take turns helping the family. We cry with their heartaches—a wayward child, lost job, foreclosed home. But, we rejoice with their happiness—a new grandbaby, promotion, college degree. We grow to love each other because we build common bonds, and Paul compares that relationship to how our own body performs. Like our natural body, the church body is comprised of members all working together (see 1 Cor. 12:14).

With our physical bodies, we cherish each part from toes to hair. We not only pamper that body but also care for its health and fix it when it hurts. We love our natural bodies, and that concept applies to our church body. Too often, our own agendas cause us to forget we're members of the same body, both of the individual and collective church. In that church, God spells out offices to be filled, which make our body complete: "God has appointed these in the church: first apostles, second prophets, third teachers, after that miracles, then gifts of healings, helps, administrations, varieties of tongues" (1 Cor. 12:28). Whether our position in the body is for prophecy, ministry, teaching, exhorting, giving, ruling, or showing mercy, each is important to the body, and none takes precedence (see Rom. 12:4-8). However, Paul doesn't stop at church offices but also lists Holy Spirit's gifts, which should be operating in His church, the body.

Body Ministry

Whether we're using revelation, speaking, or power gifts, body ministry is Holy Spirit's way of developing a picture of needs. When we move in the gifts, bit by bit He creates a complete message. I've heard it described this way: Holy Spirit is an orchestra leader; we're varied instruments in that orchestra. When everyone plays his part, it's a beautiful symphony. When one doesn't do his job, it breaks down. Another analogy is that Holy Spirit's revelations are like a jigsaw puzzle made up of abundant pieces. One piece might be a vision, one a word of knowledge, another discernment of spirits, and often each is given by someone different. Interpretations come when pieces fit together to make a picture of what Holy Spirit is revealing. When one bit of the puzzle is missing, not only is the final picture incomplete, but putting other pieces together during the process is harder.

The church in Corinth didn't understand how the gifts worked, so Paul used the comparison to the body so they could comprehend. We're each a member, and Christ is the head. "For as the body is one and has many members, but all the members of that one body, being many, are one body, so also is Christ" (1 Cor. 12:12). Gifts work through individuals who are part of the same body (see 1 Cor. 12:12-31), and they're all important. I recently attended a conference after I'd bruised the bottom of my foot. Though my foot doesn't contribute to my body's life and death, that pain affected my weekend—how I worshiped, how long I could stand in services, how I dressed, where I parked, if I could work out in the hotel gym, and whether I wanted to make that long trip to the ice machine. When we're a body, we feel each other's needs, and everything we do is to the benefit or detriment of the entire body. Thus, the church should understand and invest in body ministry.

How does it work? Basically, the "hip bone's connected to the...." Get the picture? We're attached to each other and, by extension, the whole body. Paul describes it like this:

> *From whom the whole body, joined and knit together by what every joint supplies, according to the effective working by which every part does its share, causes growth of the body for the edifying of itself in love* (Ephesians 4:16).

We're all part of this body, joined together, supplying what one another needs so we work and grow properly. The body thrives because it loves itself, doesn't do what isn't good for the whole body, and realizes the value of each member's unique purpose. It works effectively because the toe knows it can't provide what the finger does, but the whole body knows it hurts when that toe has a nail that's ingrown. If every member were an eye, how would we hear? If every member were an ear, how could the body smell (see 1 Cor. 12:17)? We're created with our own purpose for this body; whatever our job is, it's important. Because we understand our own bodies, the application to our spiritual body makes sense.

In Action

When I was young, we attended a church that operated amazingly in body ministry. Sometimes entire services were given to the operation of gifts through that ministry. People would have revelations of various puzzle parts—an ominous feeling, colors, a sky, a specific airline logo, a map pinpointing a certain location, people crying. It all added up when someone said his/her son was leaving the next day on that airline to that very city. God's warning to pray about the issue was loud and clear because the body contributed revelation about the well-being of one of its members. Paul describes how this works: "How is it then, brethren? Whenever you come together, each of you has a psalm, has a teaching, has a tongue, has a revelation, has an interpretation. Let all things be done for edification" (1 Cor. 14:26). Though our roles vary, each revelation matters to the clarity of the overall message and thus the outcome of the God-revealed issue.

Body ministry happens naturally as the body's different parts—finger, elbow, toe—occupy their places and make the revelation come into focus. As various people get words from Holy Spirit, Paul admonishes that "if anything is revealed to another who sits by, let the first keep silent" (1 Cor. 14:30). Though this Scripture deals specifically with prophecy, it's also informative about how body ministry works. First, it's for all members to contribute what God has given. But it's also to be orderly—if someone else receives a revelation, another should defer to him. One by one, parts of the body contribute; by that, others learn about the gifts while those revelations bring results that free, encourage, and empower.

We're all crucial parts of the body. This was demonstrated one morning when we pastored. I was at the keyboard facing Lucy when God gave me a vision of someone standing behind her in the pew and putting his fingers in Lucy's ears. I felt led to ask William, whose excitement to be used of God far exceeded his diminutive stature. I caught his eye, motioned for him, and asked him to anoint her ears with his fingers in both sides, just like I'd seen in the vision. Though this was a strange request, he complied. Later in the service, I saw Lucy acting like something was bothering her. Before Wade's sermon's end, she raised her hand and testified—her ears had improved so much she had needed to turn her hearing aids down dramatically.

That miracle coming to pass wasn't a job for one body member. William and I, plus others sitting around Lucy, acted and prayed, causing manifestation of the miracle.

Where You Fit

Every gift-operating, Spirit-filled believer has encountered—or will encounter—leadership that balks at operating in the gifts. Two choices exist—find another church where you can use your gifts or stay put and work within those confines. Those who feel led to remain at a church that doesn't promote the gifts can find other venues, like outside Bible studies or prayer groups, where they can still move in the Spirit. If you do stay, maybe God has a reason. Once, I attended a church with little leeway to practice my gifts. In a dream God revealed that I was planting a few seeds then moving away and later planting more. That's just what happened when God gave me revelations to share from time to time. At a different church, though, I dreamed they didn't want what I had to offer so I should find a church where I could use what He'd given.

God "covenanted with [His people] when [they] came out of Egypt, so [His] Spirit remains among you" (Hag. 2:5). That covenant of Holy Spirit was given from the beginning, but now He doesn't dwell in a tabernacle but has come to dwell in us. His gifts are our covenant right, and every body of believers should include Holy Spirit's operation. Just like the church cherishes those with technical abilities, food-preparation prowess, or organizational skills, so the church needs those who operate in the Spirit. Each church can find what works within its body so every service has a purpose and provides a time for the gifts. If a Sunday morning crowd is more suited to the salvation message, then choose prophetic altar ministers to pray for those coming forward. That brief prophetic message from God can be an amazing tool to woo the lost.

Love

Love is the motivation for Holy Spirit's gifts. If we love our brothers like our own bodies, we're courteous and tender toward one another (see 1 Pet. 3:8). If our finger is caught in the door or our toe is stubbed, the whole body hurts. If a foreign object invades our body, the entire body fights against it. Loving all the body perfects our love for one another to get rid of "divisions [and] be perfectly joined together in the same mind and in the same judgment" (1 Cor. 1:10). When we work independently from the rest of the body, we disagree about everything from our Bible version preference to who sits where. It's hard to operate properly when we have arguments with our own body. God reveals things about one another because as one body we work in love for the same goal—kingdom expansion. As we encourage one another through love's bond, we grow in God's riches.

We aren't lone rangers. We need each other because "There is one body and one Spirit, just as you were called in one hope of your calling" (Eph. 4:4). This body lifts me up when my head is weary. It suffers with me or shines when I do because I don't excel without the rest of my body (see 1 Cor. 12:26). This body gets out of bed in the middle of the night to intercede when Holy Spirit quickens that a member of its body is hurting or needs to avoid a snare. God has set us in our places to love and help one another and thus please Him. We not only must keep our spot but not denigrate others' jobs because we need each other, especially the weaker and less honorable ones (see 1 Cor. 12:18, 21-23). We matter to each other's well-being, and love makes it all work.

Conclusion

Before Wade and I married, I was a single mother attending a church with activities for my girls but no opportunity for me to utilize Holy Spirit's gifts, which longed to be used. When God led me to another church that did operate in Holy Spirit, those gifts that had lain dormant for so long felt like they had atrophied, like an inactive leg or arm. The more I used them, the more they wanted to be used. Something in me needed to operate in the gifts because they were my essence, just like my heart or my fingernail. It's taken a long time for those gifts to develop fully, but I never could have advanced in the gifts' operation if I hadn't found a body that allowed liberty to exercise those Holy Spirit limbs again.

Holy Spirit's gifts are our substance, just like each member of our physical body, and they long to be used. If we neglect them, they cry out because they're part of us, and we're part of the larger Body of Christ, which also tremendously needs them in order to profit (see 1 Cor. 12:7). So why is this body ministry important? We're a work in progress, and Holy Spirit's job is to perfect and equip us as we edify the Body of Christ (see Eph. 4:12). Holy Spirit's gifts function to bring us into the unity of the faith, to know Christ better, to have Him formed fully, and to grow up in Him (see Eph. 4:16). That growth creates stability, and every*body* needs that.

Part I

REVELATION GIFTS

REVELATION GIFTS

Wade

Every soldier needs his orders specified. The standard military operations order begins with a concise statement of the situation describing the enemy's disposition, strength, weapons placement, reserve estimates, lines of supply and communication, strengths, and weaknesses. The Lord's army is supplied with data that allows them to combat the enemy's strengths and capitalize on his weaknesses. Holy Spirit's revelation gifts provide this information through words of knowledge, words of wisdom, and discernment of spirits. All these are bestowed to Spirit-filled believers so we know "the wiles of the devil" (Eph. 6:11), to destroy his works, and to expand God's kingdom. As a matter of fact, His promise is that "secret things belong to the Lord our God, but those things which are revealed belong to us and to our children forever, that we may do all the words of this law" (Deut. 29:29). Revelation is the initiator for God's will being accomplished. Once we receive His revelation, we own it forever. How awesome is that?

The world is fascinated with the future. Millions are wasted on fortunetellers with Ouija boards, crystal balls, tarot cards, and other things employing familiar spirits, opening a door to demonic oppression and possession. All this is counterfeit, a Holy Spirit imitation. Only God reveals true knowledge and wisdom; He entrusts His valued revelation to His people, but not just to anyone. We'd never relinquish

our most precious possessions—our children, cars, financial information—to anyone who hasn't proven his worth. Solomon says, "It's the
glory of God to conceal a matter, but the glory of kings to search
out a matter" (Prov. 25:2). God desires to reveal, but revelation comes
with our diligently proving how much we want and regard it as precious treasure. Jeremiah explains, "And you will seek Me and find Me,
when you search for Me with all your heart" (Jer. 29:13). We receive
Holy Spirit's revelation to the degree we seek Him.

Obedience

God's communication may be about an assignment or special
promise, but His revelation requires proper response—hearing and
obeying. Children often have selective hearing, missing directives
when they involve cleaning their rooms or taking out the trash. They
hear just fine, though, when a trip to Dairy Queen is mentioned.
We tend to be the same with God's instructions. When we prove
ourselves trustworthy, Holy Spirit's revelation knowledge becomes
true treasure (see Matt. 6:19-21).

I like Graham Cooke's description of revelation in *A Divine
Confrontation*. He said, "Revelation is an investment of God into a
human being, and He wants a return on it—hundredfold, sixtyfold,
or thirtyfold."[1] Another favorite saying of mine comes from Pastor
Cleddie Keith at Heritage Fellowship in Florence, Kentucky. He
once said the "consolation of isolation is revelation." Time spent in
solitary communion with God is rewarded by divine revelation.

Serpent on the Pole

Far too many believers are satisfied with second- and third-hand
revelation, even from past generations. Moses fashioned a bronze
serpent on the pole, which was held up before people bitten by poi-
sonous snakes; when they looked at the serpent, they lived (see Num.
21:4-9). That serpent was a revelation and mighty miracle move of

God for that generation and was even mentioned by Jesus: "And as Moses lifted up the serpent in the wilderness, even so must the Son of Man be lifted up, that whoever believes in Him should not perish but have eternal life" (John 3:14-15). Have you ever wondered what happened to that bronze serpent? Did you know people burnt incense and worshiped that snake on a stick for over fifteen generations? When Hezekiah began to rule Judah:

He removed the high places and broke the sacred pillars, cut down the wooden image and broke in pieces the bronze serpent that Moses had made; for until those days the children of Israel burned incense to it, and called it Nehushtan (2 Kings 18:4).

Not only did Judah worship the symbol (idol) of a past move of God, they named it as well. Holy Spirit once impressed me that when a name is placed on a move of God, its ability to expand and move forward becomes limited. I believe monuments have been erected to past moves of God where men formed a circle, dug in their heels, and said, "Thus far and no farther," while Holy Spirit moved on. Without Holy Spirit's revelation and power, an animal head may as well be erected in front of churches to mark them as just another fraternal organization doing good things. Without Holy Spirit, we'll accomplish only good things, not God's things. We need modern-day Hezekiahs to release people from their worship of idols of God's past revelations and previous moves so they experience His presence today.

Holy Spirit rarely does things the same way twice. We all like predictability, but God wants total reliance upon Him when it comes to kingdom manifestations. Holy Spirit is never confined to a formula—only to kingdom principles, something God Himself initiated. Isaiah gave a heads-up regarding the nature of revelation: "Behold, the former things have come to pass, and new things I declare; before they spring forth I tell you of them" (Isa. 42:9). He also wrote, "Do not remember the former things, nor consider the things of old. Behold, I will do a new thing, now it shall spring forth;

shall you not know it? I will even make a road in the wilderness and rivers in the desert" (Isa. 43:18-19). How much do you desire Holy Spirit's revelation? Would you fast and pray to receive His direction, or are you satisfied living off moldy manna of past generations? Do you worship around a set of God's footprints—where He was years, decades, or centuries past—or are you pursuing His presence with desperation that won't be denied?

The Keys

God's always broadcasting, but we're not always tuned in to His frequency. The first key to receiving revelation is renewing the mind (see Rom. 12:1-2). This process occurs through both studying Scripture and allowing Holy Spirit to illuminate His truth. As minds are renewed through the Word, carnal nature and worldly ways of thinking become replaced with Christ's mind. In the renewing process, a person's perspective changes, going from *see level*—where he believes only what he perceives through the five natural senses (carnal mind)—to an elevated position of being "seated in the heavenly places in Christ Jesus" (Eph. 2:6). Elevation transfers believers from the illusionary, temporal environment (see 2 Cor. 4:18) into the eternal, invisible realm of Holy Spirit where they gain *vision* based upon God's truth.

The second key to receiving revelation is the intensity with which we pursue our answer. The degree of desperation one has for God determines His response. Those who "diligently seek" (Heb. 11:6) God with their whole heart receive His revelation (see Jer. 29:12-13). Too many foster a casual relationship with the Lord with this attitude, "If the Lord wanted me to know, He'd tell me." We see too many Brylcreem Christians who treat their relationship with God just like the marketing slogan of the old hair dressing commercial, "A little dab'll do ya." Perhaps lack of persistence in receiving revelation is why much of today's church is bereft of the miraculous, settling for a type of godliness but rejecting Holy Spirit's power (see 2 Tim. 3:5). Just how much do you desire His revelation?

We've witnessed amazing miracles as we entered into the kingdom principle of pursuit—asking, seeking, and knocking (see Luke 11:9-13). The Greek word for *ask* is *aiteo*, which means to "ask, beg, call for, crave, desire, require."[2] The next level of pursuit is seeking, *zeteo*, meaning "to worship (God)…desire, endeavor…require."[3] The final degree of pursuit is to knock, or *krouo*.[4] This word carries the meaning of rapping on a door to be opened, much like the man who knocked with importunity on his friend's door at midnight for food when the man and his family were in bed. The man opened because of his friend's persistence (see Luke 11:8). God desires our pursuit of Him. In fact, we attain His revelation and appropriate His covenant promises to the degree we pursue His presence. No formula or substitute exists for our desire to be in His presence and pursue His will for our lives.

Knowing Your Revelation Gifts

You'll hear us say often in this book that you should get to know how Holy Spirit uses His gifts in your life because each of us ministers differently by God's design. When Connie first began operating in the gifts, God gave her multiple revelations. What took time, though, was for her to learn how each type of revelation worked. She discovered that when God gave her a vision—for example, of someone's eye—she knew to pray for the eye but wasn't certain which one. However, when Holy Spirit gave her a pain or a specific feeling as a word of knowledge, she was certain about the location that needed healing. That understanding came through experience. For me, revelation often comes as an impression, unction, or a *certain knowing* that a condition exists and Holy Spirit is there to deliver, heal, and restore. Another initiator triggering Holy Spirit revelation for me is when I hear someone speak or look into a person's eyes. Yours may function differently; but as you operate and learn about your own wonderful administration of revelatory gifts, you become more effective in building the Kingdom.

Conclusion

When something's going to happen, God tells His prophets so others can be prepared. Amos declared, "Surely the Lord God does nothing, unless He reveals His secret to His servants the prophets" (Amos 3:7). Divine revelation is the key that initiates speaking and power gifts. As Holy Spirit reveals words of knowledge, words of wisdom, or discernment of spirits, we act on them through speaking and power gifts to bring about kingdom manifestations. Though it's important to recognize how all gifts operate, understanding revelation gifts is especially crucial because revelation is where others often begin.

How important is divine revelation? Jesus said that man does not live just by bread but by every word spoken from God's mouth (see Matt. 4:4). That "proceeding word," the *rhema*, is spoken into believers' hearts by Holy Spirit. Rhema causes faith to come on the scene (see Rom. 10:17) while providing direction, timing, and God's power (*dunamis*) to cause kingdom manifestations. If Jesus Christ acknowledged revelation's life-giving power, don't you think it's important enough to pursue with all your might? I certainly do, and I can't live victoriously without it.

WORDS OF KNOWLEDGE

Connie

One way God reveals His will is through a word of knowledge telling about a past or present event. This exciting gift is a *rhema*—God's now word to meet a need or give direction. People refer to this as "reading someone's mail" because of the incredible insight into lives. This amazing overcoming tool changes people, but it can also make us unpopular with those who don't want us to know their secrets. God reveals this so we can understand "the knowledge of the mystery of God, both of the Father and of Christ, in whom are hidden all the treasures of wisdom and knowledge" (Col. 2:2-3). That *treasure* is ours for the asking in Holy Spirit.

Responses

People's responses to words will vary. Sometimes, mouths drop open while they exclaim, "Who told you that?" One morning, I was on the ministry team at church when Jan slipped into my line. As I prayed, I saw a vision of her laughing and running in a field of green wheat. God said simply, "It's not yet time for the harvest." She burst into boisterous tears. She'd been diligently praying for a need that week when, as she drove down the street, God spoke into her heart, "It's not yet time for the harvest." That morning, God gave necessary confirmation.

Another time, service was nearly over when I felt drawn to a young mother behind me. I'd noticed her a few times but didn't know her name or anything about her. At first, I thought I was supposed to pray at our seats when the pastor gave the ministry call, but God said to ask her to go forward. I risked her saying no, especially since she didn't know me, but my job was to obey Holy Spirit. When the pastor asked us to stand, I turned and told her what I felt. She initially hesitated, but she said okay and asked me to go with her. Her eyes teared when the other minister and I prayed and gave words of knowledge. Later, she said she'd felt like going forward for several weeks and again that morning but was too shy. She'd just told the Lord if He wanted her to go to have someone else tell her; then I turned around. Sharing words of knowledge lets people realize their lives are important to God.

That's not how everyone reacts, though. We'd all like people to jump at each revelation, but often the opposite will occur. Paul's thorn in the flesh came because satan wanted to fight his rhema (see 2 Cor. 12:7). Keep in mind that when you share words of knowledge, each revelation has potential for trouble because the enemy doesn't want revelation given. Whether you're fought by a skeptic or even by trials through people who love you, Paul warned to "recall the former days in which, after you were illuminated, you endured a great struggle with sufferings" (Heb. 10:32). He understood that with revelation (illumination) come trials (struggles). Many of us have been there, done that.

Biblical Examples

Words of knowledge occur throughout the Bible. As Mary approached Elizabeth when they were both pregnant, by Holy Spirit's revelation Elizabeth knew her cousin was carrying God's Son (see Luke 1:41). When Jesus told Peter and other fishermen that casting their nets to the boat's right side would produce a great catch, He spoke through a word of knowledge (see Luke 5:4). When the new baby was brought to Anna, she reinforced that He was truly the awaited Messiah through a word of knowledge (see Luke 2:38). After Saul's Damascus Road experience, Ananias received a word of knowledge that confirmed Saul's conversion (see Acts 9:10-18).

My favorite word of knowledge story is from Jesus' ministry. Just like today, when people debate prophetic validity, Jesus was constantly challenged. Once, Nathanael had been sitting beneath a fig tree when an excited Philip told him Jesus was the Messiah. Nathanael couldn't believe it because Jesus was from a less-than-desirable city, and "Can anything good come out of Nazareth?" (John 1:46). Can't you imagine this discussion today? Can anything good come from that city, college, family, occupation? But Jesus changed Nathanael's opinion when, as he approached the Lord, Jesus made a statement. When Nathanael asked, "How do You know me?" (John 1:48), Jesus replied, "Before Philip called you, when you were under the fig tree, I saw you" (John 1:48). This incident mirrors my experiences. As a result of Holy Spirit's revelation, people are changed.

Knowledge

The Greek for words of knowledge is *gnosis*, which means "knowing (the act)…knowledge, science."[1] References exist to gnosis as spiritual words of knowledge and as literal knowledge. Paul uses this word in 1 Corinthians 8:1 when he explains how people tried to settle a doctrinal dispute with logic rather than love toward one another. He also uses the word in 1 Corinthians 12:8 when he discusses the gifts, "For to one is given the word of wisdom through the Spirit, to another the word of knowledge through the same Spirit." Paul's usages are far apart—one deals with logical knowledge, the other with spiritual knowledge. However, that duality describes us. We're flesh and blood men and women who allow the Spirit to work as revelation planted into our spirits comes into our physical minds, giving access to spiritual revelations.

Words of knowledge provide much for Spirit-filled Christians. They enrich lives and give understandable revelations (see 1 Cor. 1:5;

2:10). They make us conquerors (see 2 Cor. 10:4-5). Those words are beautiful smelling. Like a costly perfume, Holy Spirit "through us diffuses the fragrance of His knowledge in every place" (2 Cor. 2:14). Think of that. Through us, God brings that beautiful fragrance everywhere we go, and the gnosis knowledge creates the sweet savor of God. When you come into a room, do you bring Holy Spirit's fragrance?

We're Different

From DNA to hair follicles, everyone and everything is different, and the same applies to gifts. Though a limited number exists, every person "has his own gift from God, one in this manner and another in that" (1 Cor. 7:7). Once, a friend had a vision about one vine growing with other vines attached, each containing multicolored leaves. Those leaves represented the gifts. We come from the same vine and even have the same gifts, but our gifts operate differently with each person's own nuance of color. Others' gifts aren't like mine, nor are mine like theirs, by God's design. It's "one and the same Spirit [who] works all these things, distributing to each one individually as He wills" (1 Cor. 12:11).

Because gifts function differently, controversy may occur. Once, Wade and I visited a church and received several words of knowledge resulting in miracles. One woman still tells how Holy Spirit gave me such a specific word about her pain that though she hadn't witnessed words of knowledge before, she knew the revelation was for her. She responded, and her excruciating pain was healed. Later, someone from that church told me I was faking that gift. I was stunned.

"Well, not exactly faking it," he said, "because you believe it yourself. But my pastor hears from God, and he said how you get messages isn't how that works." Though administrations of gifts, ministries, activities, and forms differ, it's the same Spirit working His way. Although we must determine if someone is legitimately operating in the Spirit, no one can judge another's administration of the gifts or even choose how Holy Spirit decides to use us. I'm glad He determines who does what and how because He's so much smarter than we are.

How It Operates

Because of people's varied administrations of the gifts, covering every possibility for how someone may receive a word of knowledge is impossible. The main ways God communicates through words of knowledge are unctions, visions, and dreams (usually words of wisdom). I'll talk more about these later in this revelation section. How people receive words of knowledge varies from person to person or revelation to revelation. Sometimes, revelation comes through a simple word we either see, hear, or feel, though we may not know what it means. For instance, God once spoke *synapse* to me. A lady raised her hand immediately, eyes wide. Her young child had been to a doctor, who told her the girl's problems were with her synapses. The lady had never heard that word before, so she was shocked when God spoke it to me. Words of knowledge let people see God's majesty and care for them.

Like with our physical bodies, we become accustomed to how our gifts work. My mother, a William Branham follower in the fifties, said he once told them that when his hand tingled, he knew an angel was there for a miracle. You'll discover other ways of revelation by trial, error, and experience as words of knowledge are revealed to you. When a tingling or oil comes in my hands, I know God's going to do a miracle. Sometimes my palms get so hot they're uncomfortable as I lay them on someone. When that happens, God wants to infuse healing power into that person.

Wade and I also both get words about needs by feeling another person's physical sensation. One day, before Wade preached a funeral in Hamilton, Ohio, we were talking to a pastor. The longer we stood beside him, the worse my back felt. Finally, I turned to that pastor, put my hand on my back where I was hurting, and asked if he had back problems. Tearfully, he nodded. He'd come home early that day from vacation because his back had been bothering him so badly. As we prayed, the pain stopped.

This aspect of experiencing pain of people near me has proven itself time and again. I sometimes feel it for someone at the next table in a restaurant, in the pew beside me, or even as I write on Facebook. I really appreciate this administration of words of knowledge because it's precise. I've heard scoffers denigrate words of knowledge by saying that having an accurate word is an accident or people getting lucky and guessing what to pray for. That statement shows inexperience with how Holy Spirit works; but even if that were true, this administration of this gift tells exact symptoms and location. Arguing with that is difficult.

Common Mistakes

When you first begin to minister in your gifts, you'll make many mistakes. You didn't walk, type, or do anything perfectly when you first began. Through experience and more mature Christians, Holy Spirit encourages, mentors, teaches, and guides believers into operating more accurately. For this reason, a safe place should exist for you to make mistakes and not be devastated by others condemning you. Though errors can happen because you share incomplete revelations or misinterpretations, you may also regret when you don't give what you feel and someone suffers because of your disobedience.

As a new user of gifts, you're insecure. *What if no one responds? What if it's just me? What if people think I'm a false prophet?* Satan whispers those doubts to everyone, even seasoned veterans, because he intends to keep God's children bound in current situations from which a word of knowledge could free them. Often, though, especially when you first operate in the gifts, you'll receive confirmation, which builds confidence. Even lack of response doesn't mean the need wasn't there. People may not acknowledge that the word's for them for many reasons. They may never have witnessed the operation of words of knowledge, so they don't know how to react. Other factors may explain why they didn't come forward—embarrassment, insecurity, privacy. Usually, though, people don't want to miss that opportunity for God's touch. We've had people even come to our house after service and ask if it was too late to get that miracle.

Another reason for a lack of response is that people misunderstand what you're asking. Once Wade and I were having a service in Arizona when God gave me a word about someone's jaw. That revelation was specific, so I pointed to the location and told how it felt. No one responded. I'd been operating in my gift long enough to know the person was there regardless of the acknowledgement. We waited for a moment then continued the service.

Going home that night, my mother said, "I had something on my face, but you said 'jaw' and it's my chin."

I looked at her. "Mom, does it feel like"—whatever the symptoms were—"and is it right here?" I pointed to the spot where I'd felt pain.

"Yes," she said. Despite her not going forward and my not saying it specifically enough, she was healed on the way home. That isn't the only time people didn't respond because I'd explained it wrong, though. You learn through experience, and multiple mistakes come with that.

Receiving

Another common mistake is not receiving God's words when someone speaks them. Even when that word is right on, sometimes people either can't or won't see how it applies to them. I've given words to people who said, "No, I don't know what that is," then dismissed it rather than seeking an application for their lives. Others, however, say, "I don't know what it is right now, but I'll pray and see what God is saying." Those people get their answer because—like the Bereans who received the word from Paul then searched it out for themselves (see Acts 17:10-11)—they don't discount revelation just because they don't understand it.

As receivers of prophetic words, we should hear with an open mind but never act on any single person's revelation until Holy Spirit confirms it. Not only as a receiver but also as a giver of words, we don't want someone to respond to our word when it's the only revelation he/she has received. One seer alone shouldn't influence anyone's decisions because we're all humans, learning about our gifts. However, even if the word is imperfect, we should be open-minded and let Holy Spirit confirm or refute it, not us.

That concept became personal to me. It was nearly Thanksgiving when I realized my left big toe was numb; the last time I could remember feeling it was in the spring. I took off the polish and discovered a black vertical line under the nail from the bottom toward the top. When Wade insisted I see a podiatrist, I thought I'd probably hear I'd smashed it, so I was taken aback when the doctor returned from reading my X-rays. Several possibilities existed, he said; the most serious was melanoma. He made an appointment for more tests and possible surgery.

As I drove home to tell Wade, fear tried to creep into my spirit. Cancer—that word makes even the most spiritual react. But as satan tried bringing fear, I felt God telling me it would be okay. As my appointment drew closer, I felt even more convinced, so I cancelled. I stood on that word He'd whispered—"I'm going to heal your toe." Whenever fear tried to settle in again, I told God I trusted Him, and I prayed He'd let someone see that need through a word of knowledge. It hadn't happened during services the following couple weeks; but I waited, certain He'd come through. I thought Sunday might be my night.

The crowd was small at our little country church nestled among Indiana cornfields. It had been one of those meetings when Holy Spirit takes over and people minister to others. I waited for someone to call out my need that only Wade and I knew; but service was nearing the end, and no one had approached. Sitting at the keyboard in front of the massive stained-glass window, I'd closed my eyes when a tap on my arm made me turn and look into Herb's face. Short and thin, he probably would have been easy to take in an arm-wrestling match, yet that man was a giant in hearing from God. His tilted head and squinted eyes told me he was hearing from Him then.

Without any hoopla, he pursed his lips and said in his Southern Indiana accent, which put a couple syllables into my name, "Hey, Con, God told me your finger needs healed."

His words made me smile despite my eyes tearing and bottom lip quivering. I shook my head. He seemed confused until I said, "It's not my finger. It's my toe, and God sent you for my healing."

I removed my shoe and sock. In his humble, focused way, he stuck his finger in anointing oil and touched it to my toe. His prayer wasn't dynamic, but his few words reached a power source in the heavenlies. Herb was an imperfect vessel giving an imperfect word, but God answered it perfectly. Beginning the next morning, my previously numb toe hurt like it had an ingrown nail. All day at work that pain reminded me God was busy on my behalf. As my toenail grew out over the coming months, so did the black line until it was gone. Herb's obedience to pursue his flawed word and my receiving that word made the difference in the outcome, maybe my life.

Hard Words

When you're a seer, you're responsible for what God entrusts to you. Receiving from Holy Spirit isn't just your privilege; it's also a God-ordained responsibility. Jeremiah 23:28 says, "The prophet who has a dream, let him tell a dream; and he who has My word, let him speak My word faithfully." Belshazzar made a great feast and used vessels his father had taken from God's temple. After this, a hand appeared and wrote on the wall, so they sent for Daniel to interpret this hard word to Belshazzar—his days were numbered, he was found wanting, and his kingdom would fall. Though the words were negative and Daniel's consequences for speaking them could have been tragic, he still interpreted for the king, who not only accepted the prophecy but rewarded Daniel (see Daniel 5).

You should use wisdom but not avoid telling a hard word. Once God gave me a word for a woman I dearly loved, "It's time to get your life in order." I knew she struggled with organizational skills, so

I initially balked, not wanting to speak a hard word that was also my opinion. Integrity says if a chance exists that your word may be influenced by your opinion, you shouldn't give it as God's word. However, often God will give a confirmation that He really has spoken to you. That time, I didn't call her, but she called me.

When I told her what God had said, she replied, "That's not a hard word." She was dating a man she loved who told her he wanted to marry her after she put her life in order. When the Lord gives a word, you must go not only in wisdom and love but also in boldness. Your words could make the difference.

It's God

We must never forget gifts come from God. Let's face it. Hearing from Him and sharing liberating revelations with another is the biggest high imaginable. However, because we're human, pride can creep in. We'll operate in love and humility if we remember God is the Giver and Teacher (see John 14:26). Great men of God have forgotten that lesson and ultimately fell. No matter how hard we try on our own, none of us receive revelation without Him. We know nothing but what God's Spirit freely lets us know.

With our revelatory gifts, we're special—called people whom others often seek out. Some who operate in the gifts may become puffed up as others rely on them to hear from God. But knowing it's His will to help people and that He chooses us to accomplish the work is a humbling honor to be cherished. It has nothing to do with our abilities but rather Holy Spirit's, coupled with our willingness and obedience. We're God's emissaries to bring illumination into others' lives, just like He brought light into the earth and into our hearts (see 2 Cor. 4:6). It's God!

Conclusion

Wade once told me about how he received words of knowledge through the gift of suffering, and I said I didn't want revelation that way. However, I now see it as another precious example of God's riches (see Rom. 11:33)! As a hearer of an operator in prophetic words, no matter how you receive those treasures, you should remember several things. If God gives you revelation, you need to do something with it. Revelation needs obedience; the more faithful you are to act, the more revelations you'll receive. At times, you'll feel insecure about using your gifts. That's how we feel about everything we ultimately understand—our new stove, the machine we've recently been put on in our factory job, the cappuccino maker we got for Christmas, the new program on our computer. Wanting it, submitting to be used, obeying, then practicing and learning more about Holy Spirit's abilities bring wondrous results. Manifestations of Holy Spirit's words are wonderful weapons for overcoming, and that's the kind of knowledge all of us need.

UNCTIONS

Connie

D o you ever have *that* feeling? You can't explain it; you don't know why; but from out of nowhere, you think of it and can't get it off your mind. All you know for sure is that it's from the Lord and it's right. My mother used to say, "You just know in your knower." Sound familiar? This type of revelatory gift where you just *know* is one way God gives abundant revelations—unctions. Because they don't come with a great shaking of the earth, people often downplay these revelations; but if you become sensitive to them, they're an amazing part of your victorious lifestyle. Some call them "a feeling." Some say they're "a check in my spirit," others, "a knowing." Some say, "God whispered in my ear." Others assert, "Somethin' told me." However you label it, it's those times when you don't know how you know, but you just do. That's Holy Spirit doing His work to give a heads up. It's a word of wisdom or knowledge—an unction.

Unctions

First Kings 19 is the definitive chapter about unctions. Despite wondrous miracles God had done through him, Elijah experienced extreme discouragement. I can relate to times when even though Holy Spirit has worked mightily through me, despondency creeps in and steals the wonder. That happens to all of us, for with great victories come great trials. Elijah wanted to hear from God and looked for mighty ways He'd speak—a great wind, earthquake, fire (see 1 Kings 19:11-12). Yet, God chose to communicate with Elijah in a "still small voice" (1 Kings 19:12).

The word for *still* is *demamah*, meaning "calm, silence,"[1] the sound of "a delicate, whispering voice."[2] Don't you love that description? That unction doesn't hit you like a marching band, just a "delicate whispering." In verse 13, Elijah covered his face to reverence God's stillness. This says God's communication is important, whether loud or quiet. You must be in awe of His word—written, audible, visual, the sound of many waters, or just a simple unction.

God speaks in many ways. Though most of these seem more intense than unctions, that manner of revelation is just as crucial—and more common than other types of communication. Often, unctions come as a simple impression I know is right. One night, for example, our niece's son came to my mind as I felt the word *apnea* in my spirit. Neither Wade nor I knew if the boy had been diagnosed with that, so I called his mother.

"It's strange you asked that," she said. "He just stayed all night with his friend. His mom said he was breathing funny and asked if he had apnea." That revelation wasn't strange at all. God had used an unction and subsequent prayer to bring healing to a little boy.

Though many Scriptures describe how unctions work, only one uses that word. First John 2:20 says, "But you have an anointing [*unction* in KJV] from the Holy One, and you know all things." Think of those words' power. Unctions from Holy Spirit have a purpose—for us to know *all* things. I have occasional visions, dreams, or prophetic words, but I hear from God this way multiple times every day. Holy Spirit is constantly putting things into my mind—I should buy these products, not those; or I should go this route, not that one. I should give this person a little cash or hand-me-down clothes. I should go to the midweek church service no matter how tired I am. I should pray because something is going to happen. I should intercede for someone I can't get out of my mind. Do these sound familiar? Like every other gift, the key is learning to fine-tune His voice in our ears and acting in obedience.

The First John use of unction is *chrisma*, "an unguent or smearing, i.e. (fig.) endowment of the Holy Spirit: anointing."[3] I love that definition. As a Spirit-filled believer, I'm used to anointing people with oil as I pray words of faith. However, this anointing is richer. It's a salve smeared on. Think of how Vaseline covers—thickly and thoroughly. It's not a fancy lotion you pay a fortune for at the department store. It's common yet rich and thick. That's how unctions work. They're unobtrusively planted into your spirit but are powerful, rich, plentiful, and effective.

Like Other Gifts

We don't always know how God spoke to biblical prophets, but He used the same ways He speaks now, including unctions. In Acts 16, disciples were deciding where to do their next preaching. So "now when they had gone through Phrygia and the region of Galatia, they were forbidden by the Holy Spirit to preach the word in Asia" (Acts 16:6). Then they preached in Mysia, but "after they had come to Mysia, they tried to go into Bithynia, but the Spirit did not permit them" (Acts 16:7).

We don't know how Holy Spirit forbade them twice. It might have been a vision, dream, unction, word, audible voice, or maybe just circumstances that showed it wasn't His will. Often, our plans didn't work out for many reasons—doors closed, car trouble, lost directions, financial shortfalls. Though at the time we felt those were bad, they turned out to be His will to direct our actions. Sometimes loud and boisterous isn't what's called for, but rather still and small. Then He's shouting at us by just letting everything fall through.

Whether it's His directing circumstances or giving us an unction, that quiet direction can produce great results. One morning, Wade and I were visiting a church when I was drawn toward a lady near the front. God spoke to me in His small voice, "Through the lattice." As He said that, I remembered two Bible stories. First was the Song of Solomon love story where the narrator's beloved showed himself

45

through the lattice (see Song of Sol. 2:9). The other was when King Ahaziah fell through the lattice and was badly hurt (see 2 Kings 1:2). When I remembered that, I knew the enemy planned to make that woman fall. At the service's end, I asked if we could pray protection over her. Afterward, she told me her knee had given out so badly that week that she couldn't walk. A fall was a reality with a knee in such bad shape. That revelation came as an unction in three ways—as a tug toward someone, a gentle word spoken, and a knowing what God meant by those words. Another thing about it is the importance of recognizing the written Word. God took logos and made it rhema to speak into another's life.

Unctions are a perceiving, not like an audible voice or a picture in your mind. Even non-Christians have learned to follow feelings, yet this gift is often misunderstood. Many believers describe unctions as "The Lord spoke to me." That statement is sometimes confusing because others assume it's an audible voice rather than His quiet whisper into you. He's communicating gently, often out of the blue and about things not even close to what was on your mind. When it involves a person, you may think of him with a bad or good feeling and not be able to get him out of your spirit. God's giving a nudge to do something, and He'll show you what you need to know to accomplish His purpose (see John 16:13). Like other gifts, unctions may come during your busy day, but often it's when you set time apart to get still before God and listen. When you're quiet, hearing God is easier. David "meditate[d] within [his] heart, and [his] spirit [made] diligent search" (Ps. 77:6). Often, revelation has come because I stopped, listened, and searched diligently.

You Just Know

You can't explain how unctions work by the world's standards, but revelations come from God, not the world (see 1 Cor. 2:12). You grow to distinguish His voice as you become more accustomed to hearing from Him, like talking with someone on the phone. At first, you aren't sure of that person's voice; but the more times you communicate, the better you fine-tune your ability to recognize it. It's a matter of intimacy and frequency. Similarly, when the Father speaks you'll know even His quiet voice. His unction becomes the knowing in your knower. Holy Spirit possesses all knowledge, so sensitivity to and relationship with Him make the knowing alive in your spirit. Then you know you're to intercede, declare a healing, or believe for deliverance. You just know.

God often speaks into my knower by troubling my spirit. I compare it to how it bothers me when suddenly I'm disquieted and can't get something from my mind. *Did I unplug the iron? Was the stove turned off? Did I lock my desk at work?* This parallels with your Holy Spirit knowing, except that your spirit, not your mind, is troubled, so you know you need to act. It's that sword that divides the soul from the spirit and speaks into your heart (see Heb. 4:12). I compare it to 1 Kings 18:17 when Ahab called Elijah the "troubler of Israel."

The word for "trouble" is *akar*, meaning "to roil water; fig. to disturb or afflict...stir."[5] Roiling is that process of stirring water so sediment comes to the top. That reminds me of when I stayed with my friend when I was a girl. Her family lived in the country and didn't have inside plumbing, so they got drinking water from a spring out back. When a novice like me tried to dip water from the spring, the bucket touched the bottom and stirred up mud. Then we had to wait for the water to clear up again. That's how this gift works. It troubles you inside to get your attention. Then you wait until clarity comes and you receive His direction.

That happened one day when I got a message online from a friend. As I typed a response, I felt the tugging that I needed to pray for her. I stopped and saw a vision. When I told her online, she knew what it meant. When she called to tell me about it, I suddenly got a vicious pain, which she confirmed she'd been battling. When Wade and I prayed, she felt better immediately. She was amazed because that morning when she'd gotten up, God told her He'd do something good for her that day. That revelation was one of those times the troubling in my spirit made me just know I needed to pray.

Lessons

Whether Holy Spirit speaks through a disquieted spirit or vicious pain, all His revelations are important, especially to that one about whom He's speaking. When unctions come about future events, God wants you to do something. I was reminded of the necessity of listening to God's words one week when my girls were three. I'd dreamed of an evil spirit calling Jennifer's name from our basement laundry room. I prayed over her and believed God had intervened. A few days later, she was playing in the tub while Jill and I were sitting in the next room, reading. I was listening, and I thought I heard her get out; but then she was still splashing, so I figured I was wrong.

When I went into the bathroom to get her from the tub, though, I reached inside the linen closet for a towel. There on the laundry chute door was her small, wet footprint. Jennifer had sneaked from the tub, climbed shelves in the linen closet to get something, and stepped on the laundry chute door to get higher. Though I usually kept that door open, for some reason (an unction), that day I'd closed it. Had I ignored the dream and then the unction to close that door, her small body could have easily fit in the chute and plummeted onto the concrete laundry room floor below. Whatever God's saying and in whatever way He chooses, we should listen.

Confidence

Because we're Spirit-filled, many things will confirm an unction, including our knower. Don't fret because "we are of God...By this we know the spirit of truth and the spirit of error" (1 John 4:6). Unctions aren't as concrete as other ways of hearing from God, so experiences build confidence that God's speaking. That comes through times we either received confirmation of the word's validity or heard but didn't obey and lived to regret it. With each occasion when we operate in this gift, confidence grows; but we're still learning, so for now, we "know [*ginosko*, meaning to "be aware (of), feel...perceive...understand"⁴] in part and we prophesy in part" (1 Cor. 13:9). We won't know everything and are sometimes wrong; but like other gifts, we're more fine-tuned as we go. We test it and trust Him to direct us in how to proceed. If the unction was a word of wisdom (a future event), we may not know the magnitude of the revelation because we may never see what was avoided. Because of that, some people, even us, may question whether we actually heard from God. We must stand on what we know and rejoice *because* we don't see the revelation come to pass.

My sister Liz never saw the accuracy of her unction about her son, but she knew God had spared him. When he was young, she suddenly was overtaken with a burden for Zach. She called my mother to help her intercede. As they prayed, Mom saw a vision of a dragonfly and remembered that when she was young, Grandpa told them that wherever there's a dragonfly, a snake is nearby to eat it. Snakes were a reality in that Arizona environment, so my sister went to his preschool and picked him up early. She never saw the calamity God told her about, but He later put a woman in her path with whom Liz shared this incident. She teared up and told Liz about when she too had felt a burden for her son who was playing in a tree. She ignored that unction; and within minutes, her son fell from the tree, broke his neck, and died. That woman confirmed that God had saved Zach's life through Liz's obedience. Even if heeding our unctions makes us look silly or we never know what He saved us from, God's unctions have proven themselves time and again. We'd better take them seriously.

A pastor's wife from Michigan discovered the outcome when she overrode God's whisper and suffered as a result. At the store, God told her to buy a toothbrush. She thought that was silly because she'd recently bought a family supply. When she went home, though, her son had a friend there and asked if he could stay overnight. She agreed then found his guest didn't have his toothbrush. She smiled slightly as she realized God's unction had been right on. The boys asked if they could ride bikes the short distance to buy one. She received a negative Holy Spirit tug; but as she looked into her son's pleading eyes, she relented. They were gone a short time when the friend burst back into the house. Her son had wrecked his bike and broken his arm.

If this woman of God had listened when He first told her about the toothbrush, she'd have been amazed and grateful that God cared about that little boy's needs. But she never would have known He wanted to save her own son from a broken arm, which affected their upcoming Disney World vacation and his next soccer season. We may never know what pitfall we missed by following unctions; but with each revelation, we gain confidence in God's ability to care for His children, to speak in that still voice, and to nurture our sensitivity to hear that whisper. For life's complicated journey, God's given many weapons. Unctions are powerful and effective to thwart the enemy's plans for our destruction.

Conclusion

My sister Anita tells about once when she was in her twenties and having physical problems, and the doctor prescribed several drugs. Anita called our mom for prayer and told her what she was taking. Mom called back and told Anita she shouldn't take one prescription because she had a bad feeling about it. Anita knew better than to argue when Mom got that "I've-heard-from-God" tone, so she complied. Over twenty years later, Anita heard a news story about that drug—it caused horrible side-effects, including kidney failure. For all those years, the human eye may have thought Mom missed it; but Holy Spirit never, ever gets things wrong.

Right now, some of you are probably thinking you could never get specific, accurate revelations. You may feel you couldn't have confidence to say you *know* something. Even with unctions, the simplest of revelations, *you* can't, but Holy Spirit can. God "who searches the hearts knows what the mind of the Spirit is, because He makes intercession for the saints according to the will of God" (Rom. 8:27). Christ's mind is in us (see Phil. 2:5), so we can trust we're listening to the Spirit instead of our own thoughts. Like sheep, we know His voice (see John 10:4-5), and that voice sticks with us so we can't get it out of our minds. When we act on the unction, or even if we drop the ball, we can learn from those times. How amazing are quiet unctions in a believer's life! How do I know that? I just know.

VISIONS

Connie

Visions are another aspect of revelation. Those of us who have this gift are visionaries, seers, separated from the rest of the world because we see with spiritual eyes. We're *chozeh*, "a beholder in vision...prophet...seer."[1] Wow, I love that word. Another word describes our gift, *chazown*, "a sight, i.e. a dream, revelation."[2] This aspect of revelation is crucial; Solomon said that when we don't have revelation (*chazown*), we live haphazardly and unhappily (see Prov. 29:18). When we're God's *chozen*, we have direction.

Making a Place

The concept of seers, the *chozeh*, is rife throughout the Word—Abraham (see Gen. 15:1), Isaiah (see 2 Chron. 32:32), Iddo (see 2 Chron. 9:29), Jesus, and many others. Just like Old and New Testament biblical models, we receive divine revelation and direction from God, who is still speaking to His children through visions. I see frequent visions and concur with Solomon's words: "A man's gift makes room for him, and brings him before great men" (Prov. 18:16). Any of Holy Spirit's gifts—from visions to miracles—demonstrate ability to hear from God and make a niche with others. Those gifts speak to even the unsaved or those who disagree with the prophetic. Remember when ungodly kings saw how miraculously Daniel's God operated (see Dan. 5:12)? Because of his gifts, Daniel showed God's might to the unsaved and found favor with even heathens.

Once, I was visiting a gracious friend and her husband who opened their home to me. Lying in bed the night before I left for home, I asked God to give me something about a touchy situation in their lives. He did through a vision. The message was clear—they weren't seeing the whole picture. I knew my friend readily accepted words from God, but her husband was leery of the prophetic. The next morning at breakfast, I told them my vision and what God had said. As I glanced back and forth between them, I not only saw my friend's acknowledgement but also her husband's listening and accepting. They acted on that message from God; as a result, that situation that could have negatively impacted their family forever was resolved. That's the prophetic power.

Our Other Eyes

Visions work because Holy Spirit gives capability to see beyond natural senses. We possess two sets of eyes—one physical and one spiritual. Some Christians haven't learned about the "other eyes" yet; but like all things spiritual, what we see with those eyes is more real than we see with natural eyes. Elisha's servant couldn't discern spiritual reinforcements encamped around them. When Elisha prayed for his spiritual eyes to be opened, "Then the Lord opened the eyes of the young man, and he saw. And behold, the mountain was full of horses and chariots of fire all around Elisha" (2 Kings 6:17). His natural eyes had, of course, already been opened, so these were his spiritual eyes. Reality said they were in hopeless circumstances, but seeing with their other eyes showed a massive, undefeatable army.

Believing their natural rather than spiritual eyes changed a potential two-week journey[3] to a forty-year trek because of the children in the wilderness' lack of faith. Twelve spies reconnoitered the Promised Land to see if they could defeat the occupants. When reporting, ten spies said they "were like grasshoppers in [their] own sight" (Num.

13:33). Seeing circumstances from their own eyes brought fear and inability to move into their destiny. Joshua and Caleb, however, saw the enemy through spiritual eyes, so they knew they could "go up at once and take possession, for [they were] well able to overcome it" (Num. 13:30). Spiritual eyes allow us to see from God's perspective with great insight to surge forward for victory over seemingly unconquerable giants. Visions give direction for how to pray because they show revelations unseen with natural eyes to correct current problems or avoid potential ones. Visions seen with those other eyes are solid, powerful words from God.

Types of Visions

As with other gifts, visions come with varied urgency. As a seer, it's not necessary for you to know each level's name nor identify your vision type. Actually, that's difficult for me too because all are similar. Though each vision is important, the revelation's intensity—from fleeting impressions to trances—denotes a more critical need and requires more responsibility to act. Some visions are so powerful that others feel or hear them. Daniel described his vision, which others didn't see but felt such terror they ran and hid (see Dan. 10:7). When Saul had his vision on the road to Damascus, others heard but couldn't see (see Acts 9:7). Scripture records different types of visions, all of which I've experienced.

Horasis
It is the "act of gazing—an inspired appearance: sight."[4] Old Testament is *chizzayown*: "a revelation, especially by dream: vision."[5] Most visions fall into this category. Prophecy in both the Old and New Testaments refers to this vision type when Joel and Acts predicted widespread use of dreams and visions (see Acts 2:17; Joel 2:28). This is the type I most commonly experience. Often, as I minister, I see parts of bodies highlighted and know exactly where to pray. One time, God showed me an area on a woman's back and heels. When I prayed for those places, this woman was astounded. That spot I'd

seen on her back was the exact injection site where she'd been receiving shots for pain. It had been causing her great nerve discomfort in both her back and heels. She was healed that morning because that vision gave a rhema, which touched God's throne.

Optasia

It refers to a "visuality; an apparition."[6] This type of vision is stronger. For me, it's more than a horasis flash, and I see it as if it's really there. At times my eyes have been open, but usually they're closed. Often, with eyes shut, I see specific things I know are present although I can't see them in the natural. As I watch, details come into focus and the meaning becomes clear. Paul referred to this type when he said the Lord will come in visions and revelations (see 2 Cor. 12:1). This vision is used in Luke 1:22 when Zachariah saw the angel who announced John and then again in Luke 24:23 when women at Jesus' grave saw angels. An element of reality occurs in this vision type.

Once, when I was going through an extreme trial, I was awakened during the night. With eyes still closed, I saw a vision of an angel bending over me. I abruptly opened my eyes and couldn't see him; when I closed them again, my other eyes saw God's messenger so clearly I could describe his body build and his hair falling across his face. I knew he was dispatched to fight that battle for me; so like when Elisha's servant saw with his *other* eyes, I knew I could rest and receive victory. Though I'd seen visions frequently, this clarity was reserved for my extreme situation.

Horama

It means "something gazed at, i.e. a spectacle (especially supernatural); sight, vision."[7] In the Old Testament, it's *mareh*, "an appearance whether a shape or a vision…to see."[8] This type of vision is like an unfolding scenario and denotes more urgency. Some call these open visions because you're involved. Ezekiel experienced this when "the spirit took [him] up and brought [him] in a vision…into Chaldea, to those in captivity. And the vision that [he] had seen went up from [him]" (Ezek. 11:24). Another time, God took Ezekiel in a horama (mareh) into Israel and set him upon a high mountain (see Ezek. 40:2). New Testament examples also show these realistic visions. Jesus called the incident at the Mount of Transfiguration a vision (horama) to share after He had risen (see Matt. 17:19). Ananias's vision to go to Saul and Cornelius' angelic visit about Peter were horamas (see Acts 9:10-12; 10:3). I've experienced this type a few times.

One morning at the keyboard in the front, I saw Jean worshiping in the back. When I looked, she was holding a child on her hip and then wasn't, and no child was around. I watched, confused. When worship finished, I asked if she had a granddaughter about the age I'd seen. She confirmed and said she was having ear surgery. We prayed for Jean in proxy for her granddaughter. The next morning, when the girl went for the operation, she was sent home, healed. This urgent, powerful vision brought this miracle into existence.

Ekstasis

It refers to "amazed, amazement, astonishment, trance," derived from *existema*, "a displacement of the mind."[9] This most powerful type of vision, called a trance, is like that final definition—as if your mind is somewhere else. This type is mentioned several times in the New Testament. Peter's housetop revelation about animals and his later comments were called a trance (see Acts 10:10 and 11:5). God told Paul in a trance to get out of Jerusalem quickly (see Acts 22:17). Trances are reserved for dire matters.

I had my first ekstasis experience in early September 2001. I was standing in the front during Sunday-night worship. A powerful anointing came so strongly I felt my legs buckling, a sensation I called "my Gumby legs." That night, as Gumby legs crept upon me, I took a step toward the pew while I could still stand. One step was all I got before something pushed me. I knew it was an angel because no one was near. I landed with such force that my legs froze in the air. Fortunately, I'd worn capris that night! Though I still had my faculties, I couldn't move even my fingers when God began revelations. I saw an open area with birds swooping down, attacking people. As they scattered, the blackest black I'd ever seen surrounded them. I lay watching for probably thirty minutes (legs still frozen) because time had no meaning in that state. When I could move, I shared my vision. None of us had experienced anything comparable and had no idea what God was saying. We found out a few days later as birds rammed into the Twin Towers and people scattered. Along with smoke came a blackness we heard newscasters refer to as I had described—the "blackest black" they'd ever seen. That was the first but not my last trance. They always come so powerfully I can't stand up; I become immobile, unable to move a finger; and time has no relevance. After the 9/11 revelation when we didn't know how to pray, we've come against each situation and have seen amazing results.

Record It

Though visions fall into different categories, similar traits exist. As words of wisdom or knowledge, they provide insight to yours and others' lives because people hear directly from God. Moses said, "If there is a prophet among you, I, the Lord, make Myself known to him in a vision; I speak to him in a dream" (Num. 12:6). In other words, having visions or dreams makes you prophetically gifted. I'll talk about dreams later. Although God gives you a right-on word, a revelation may not come to pass immediately, so recording it lets details remain fresh until the event takes place. Habakkuk says:

> *Then the Lord answered me and said: "Write the vision and make it plain on tablets, that he may run who reads it. For the vision is yet for an appointed time; but at the end it will speak, and it will not lie. Though it tarries, wait for it; because it will surely come, it will not tarry" (Habakkuk 2:2-3).*

Especially after trance states, when I'm able to write, I record meticulous details that later add up to a message I can recall clearly even after time has passed.

Interpretations

Receiving revelation is just part of a seer's responsibility. Many aren't sure how to interpret their revelations, especially dreams and visions. They're both often symbolic (see Hos. 12:10), so their meaning doesn't fall easily upon us. Every seer doesn't always know the interpretation, nor did biblical seers. God wants us to desire understanding so badly we seriously seek it. When we're unsure about the meaning, God will show us if we truly search (see Jer. 29:13). Like everything else in our Christian walk, especially in our gifts, God rewards our yearning to get better at interpretations. Because of the symbolism, the meanings are often masked. Some symbols are generally the same, so resources are a great help. We've included a "Dreams and Visions Symbols Glossary" in the appendix of this book. I'll discuss that further in the "Dreams" chapter.

Often our visions relate to other people, so we should decide what to do with that revelation. When the Shunammite woman came to Elisha after her son's death, he didn't know what was troubling her because "the Lord ha[d] hidden it from [him], and ha[d] not told [him]" (2 Kings 4:27). God doesn't tell us everything, especially when we have a revelation about others. Maybe our vision's meaning about another person isn't for us to know; God wants the other person to seek Him; or if God told its entirety, someone may act out of His timing and negate His plans. When we don't have an interpretation, telling the revelation without venturing a guess about its meaning is crucial. Not telling what *we* think is difficult, but we can be wrong and might mislead or confuse the person who would eventually arrive at God's meaning.

When we don't understand, we should put it on the shelf. Once, when Daniel had a message for King Cyrus, "the message was true, but the appointed time was long...for the vision refer[red] to many days yet to come" (Dan. 10:1,14). We're a culture that doesn't like long appointed times—we get irritated if McDonald's service is a little slow or become impatient waiting for the microwave. We want a quick fix, but He desires us to seek Him. Usually, even those who go away without knowing the meaning later tell me God revealed it to them. In my experience, shelf time with visions is usually shorter than with dreams.

One night, I was speaking in Arizona when the Lord gave me a vision about a man. When I told him what I saw, he shook his head and said he didn't know what it meant. At times, that response is disconcerting; satan chides that others will think I'm a false prophet. That night, I didn't stutter about possible meanings, a trap I've fallen into way too often. I just told him to put it on the shelf. By service's end, he was in front crying and sharing how that vision was exactly what had been going on in his life. If I'd given my own quick spin, I may have been wrong, and he may not have arrived at God's message, which touched him so deeply.

Conclusion

Visions are precious, amazing gifts Holy Spirit has for all who seek. Sometimes their coming to pass and our knowing a revelation's fullness takes a while, but it will happen. As a young person, single mother, and now a minister with my husband, visions are an amazing part of my Holy Spirit revelatory walk that gives needed direction. Just like Paul knew his next step when he had a vision of a man from Macedonia who pleaded with him to come help them (see Acts 16:9), I rely on visions to direct my actions. Like you, sometimes my natural senses get in the way; but when I trust those other eyes, my vision is truly 20/20.

WORDS OF WISDOM

Connie

For what man knows the things of a man except the spirit of the man which is in him? Even so no one knows the things of God except the Spirit of God. Now we have received, not the spirit of the world, but the Spirit who is from God, that we might know the things that have been freely given to us by God. These things we also speak, not in words which man's wisdom teaches but which the Holy Spirit teaches, comparing spiritual things with spiritual. But the natural man does not receive the things of the Spirit of God, for they are foolishness to him; nor can he know them, because they are spiritually discerned.
—*1 Corinthians 2:11-14*

As I look over the above passage, I'm humbled and awestruck. We operators in Holy Spirit's gifts are outside our human comfort zone. Those gifts are foolishness, not just to "natural man" but unfortunately to much of the church and even to some who understand how everything works. To humans, everything Holy Spirit authors is ultimate foolishness, but prophetic beings see things differently. We know nothing except through Holy Spirit. When we tune in to Him, though, we receive abundant revelation. Once we're open to and hungry for deeper things, they're "freely given to us by God." We discern these things spiritually because we're now spiritual creatures, and rarely does anyone scoff after seeing results.

Once, when my daughters were sophomores at Indiana University, I dreamed about a situation in their lives. When my daughter told her unsaved roommate the details and the dream's message, because of its accuracy her roommate's reaction was, "No way!" When they were seniors, I again had a warning dream and felt led for Wade to anoint their rooms in the house they shared with four girls. When not only their sophomore roommate but the others found out about the dream and impending prayer, they all said, "Have your stepdad bless our rooms too!" We don't need to prove Holy Spirit's gifts; He'll prove Himself to others who may never have seen His power.

Words of Wisdom

In First Corinthians 12:8, Paul lists words of wisdom as one of the nine gifts. That word is *sophia*—"wisdom (higher or lower, worldly or spiritual)."[1] Like the meaning of knowledge, the Greek word for *wisdom* can be natural or spiritual revelation because though you hear Holy Spirit with your heart, He uses your mind to make that connection. His desire is "that the God of our Lord Jesus Christ, the Father of glory, may give to you the spirit of wisdom and revelation in the knowledge of Him" (Eph. 1:17). Think of that! God desires to give not what natural man considers wise but secrets that far surpass the world's wisdom.

I've heard two explanations for words of wisdom, and both of them are wonderful and necessary in this Holy Spirit arsenal. The first draws on the same distinction that exists between regular knowledge and wisdom. Knowledge is the collection of facts, while wisdom is knowing how to apply that knowledge. We all know those who are highly educated but aren't wise about decisions. Supernatural wisdom isn't only receiving but knowing proper application of God's gifts. Do you know when to speak or when to keep quiet? Can you accurately interpret facts God revealed? Do you understand timing and other implications that could impact God's message?

This wisdom goes beyond natural wisdom the world admires when we "have a good head on our shoulders." It's supernatural wisdom that says, "I shouldn't go there today," though logic says we bought the nonrefundable ticket and promised our best friend we'd attend. It's wisdom that comes only from God because in ourselves we couldn't or wouldn't come up with that. It's the supernatural wisdom that came to Solomon when he suggested cutting the disputed baby in half (see 1 Kings 3:25). It's that part of our spirits that just knows what to do then applies that knowing as Holy Spirit clarifies and directs. That wisdom is crucial in using revelation gifts to bring about Holy Spirit empowerment and create kingdom manifestations through speaking and power gifts.

The second way people describe words of wisdom is the one we'll primarily use in this book. While words of knowledge reveal past or present events, words of wisdom foretell future events. John describes them this way: "However, when He, the Spirit of truth, has come, He will guide you into all truth—and He will tell you things to come" (John 16:13). The "things to come" speak of words of wisdom. Because future events haven't happened yet, operating in words of wisdom requires more faith and confidence than receiving words of knowledge, which can be confirmed immediately. With words of wisdom, no concrete proof shows the event will occur; if you pray against it, nothing will probably *ever* happen because God lets that catastrophe be circumvented. Remember when my sister Liz had the unction about her son's safety? That unction was a word of wisdom, which never occurred because God intervened. Though sometimes we'll later hear a testimony, like Liz's, we usually just know God has thwarted the enemy. We gain that confidence experience by experience.

Words of wisdom are similar to words of knowledge, and revelation comes in the same forms—visions, unctions, dreams. That's why distinguishing between whether it's now or later is often difficult. After all these years of operating in both words of knowledge and wisdom, I still don't always know if the word is past, current, or future. One morning, a young mother and grandmother brought their four-year-old to my ministry line. As I prayed, pain started on my temple and up into my head. Usually when I feel pain, it's for someone around me. I asked them, even the child, if anyone hurt, but no one suffered from it. I figured someone else would show up before I left church, so I didn't pray for the girl about that. The next day, the little girl's mother sent a Facebook message that they'd gone to lunch after church. The child bent over the table and hit her head exactly where I'd felt pain. That night, she complained of a headache. If I'd prayed over her regardless of what our minds knew then as reality, that little girl would have avoided injury and pain. No one would have known God had touched her, but that's how this gift works. When nobody responds to a revelation, I now pray for anything the enemy might have planned. Even if people think we're wrong when they don't see evidence, we should trust our gifts and know God told us.

These mysteries are ordained by God instead of traditional wisdom, and confidence and revelations will grow as we do. Paul said:

> *We speak wisdom among those who are mature, yet not the wisdom of this age, nor of the rulers of this age, who are coming to nothing. But we speak the wisdom of God in a mystery, the hidden wisdom which God ordained before the ages for our glory* (1 Corinthians 2:6-7).

That revelation about the little girl wasn't earth-shattering "wisdom of this age" but was important and wisdom not defined by what the carnal mind can fathom. If we trust Holy Spirit to have all wisdom, we can proceed victoriously even if we don't logically understand. When Jesus told Peter he'd betray Him three times before morning (see Luke 22:34), He was proclaiming a word of wisdom. Had Peter seriously considered this message, perhaps the betrayal that bothered him to his death may have been avoided.

Holding on to Your Confidence

Discerning the difference between words of knowledge and wisdom will come through experience. When we pastored, Wade, many others, and I operated frequently in words of knowledge. Nearly always when God gave revelation, people came forward and we'd see immediate results. At times, though, He spoke something I knew was as important as any revelation, but no one responded. At first, I thought maybe someone was shy, which was often proven when a person came to me privately. However, sometimes the reason was that the revelation was a word of wisdom rather than knowledge.

That happened one Sunday morning when I was at the piano before church. I stood up from the bench and became so dizzy I had to grab the piano. Again, as with other revelations, intensity reflects importance. Right then, before service, I asked if anyone in the sanctuary felt like that. The only response was from one woman who said she sometimes had a little dizziness. Though we prayed for her and she was healed, I knew this was intense and debilitating, not just a little dizziness. We prayed that morning for anyone else it might include because often a revelation is for a loved one needing intercession. My dizziness left, but I still wondered about it.

I didn't ponder long, though. A couple days later, my mother-in-law called with a praise report. Her other son and his two children had moved into her country farmhouse. Somehow, her basement generator was emitting carbon monoxide. When her granddaughter walked into the house later that night, she grew dizzy; knew something was wrong; and, with difficulty, woke the other three. If God hadn't revealed satan's intentions, our family would have planned funerals. Instead, we rejoiced about God's goodness.

One Scripture best describes a word of wisdom's purpose: "Surely, in vain the net is spread in the sight of any bird" (Prov. 1:17). Don't you love that? The devil constantly tries to entrap us and our families. He'll use anything—drugs, lust, finances, even death. But Solomon reminds us that whatever satan has in store is ineffective if we see it in advance through Holy Spirit. When we know the future and pray about it, he can spread his net all he wants, but he can't snare us—his trap is "in vain." Like my dizziness experience, often a revelation may seem unimportant or confusing, but we can't allow our confidence to be jarred when the enemy is looking for every opportunity to violate us and our loved ones.

His Frequency

Because words of wisdom bring power to overcome satan's plans, warfare is slanted in our favor when God's wisdom is made known. We can war against principalities and powers (see Eph. 3:10). Because of this wisdom, our enemy has no chance against us when we battle from heavenly places. We go to war knowing we're victorious not only because of the cross but also because of a rhema that tells of the enemy's war plans. Wouldn't it be nice to go into every battle knowing not only the outcome but also full disclosure of the enemy's strategy and how to put him under our feet? We can and should! We can access spiritual wisdom because nothing that's happened or will happen is a surprise to God.

If we tune in to His frequency daily, we'll be aware of God's warning. Holy Spirit alerts us in many ways. At times, I've received these words of wisdom through my natural senses—an odor, like desert sage after an Arizona rainfall, and let me know God would soon send me on a western trip. He did several times. I've also heard sounds like a car crash or audible voice of a person for whom I was to intercede. We have Christ's mind, and Holy Spirit uses our minds and bodies to instruct us both in battles and the walk in between war times (see 1 Cor. 2:16). When our mind's channel is tuned in to God, He'll unveil what we should know.

With this gift, we speak God's mysteries He's stored up for us forever (see 1 Cor. 2:7). God has known these secrets long before man created the pyramids or Noah built his ark. These timeless revelations can now be given through words of knowledge and wisdom, all crucial to uncovering God's mystery. When Wade and I first married, he hadn't had much experience with words of wisdom, especially in dreams, and was leery of how God spoke to my family prolifically through those amazing revelations. Now he says he'd rather drive down the road on one of my dreams than in a car. These revelations are so precious even angels revere them (see 1 Pet. 1:12). Words of wisdom are crucial to our arsenal that frees and empowers.

Conclusion

"The fear of the Lord is the beginning of wisdom, and the knowledge of the Holy One is understanding" (Prov. 9:10). As we grow in intimacy with the Lord, so does our understanding of what He wants to tell us. Often, words of wisdom seem foolish to others who have natural knowledge and wisdom, but that's not Holy Spirit's wisdom. Hosea says that lack of knowledge leads to people's destruction (see Hos. 4:6). Because we don't go to God's revelatory place, we often walk through unnecessary pain and suffering from which we could have been spared by heeding words of wisdom. I can't imagine approaching tomorrow without knowing God will reveal what's necessary for my life. Want to know which road is better? Which house to buy? Which girl to marry? Which job to accept? The future is no secret if the Spirit directs. Words of wisdom and all God's revelations may seem foolish to the world, but it's wisdom that's my kind of foolishness.

DREAMS

Connie

We receive a large number of inquiries about dreams. At our Holy Spirit workshops, people are most interested in that subject. Interviews, books, and personal experiences make dreams a topic of curiosity because even the secular world understands they carry meaning. No wonder the Bible deals often with this amazing phenomenon. In my experience, dreaming is the entry into the prophetic; even children, those with little experience with the gifts, and the unsaved can dream. I can't remember a time when God hasn't directed my paths by those night visits. Both dreams and visions are crucial, simple, yet profound revelations. Dreams are often purer communications because when you're asleep, not as much of yourself is involved as when you're awake, so the revelation is not encumbered by the mind. I need that. My days are filled with "stuff," so I don't always stop to hear from God. When you're asleep, though, He speaks through dreams when your mind isn't cluttered with what your best friend is saying about you or the boss is asking you to do. Job confirmed that dreams occur during our REM deep-sleep phase when God speaks "in a dream, in a vision of the night, when deep sleep falls upon men, while slumbering on their beds" (Job 33:15). That's why sometimes the enemy interrupts your "deep sleep." He wants to steal these precious, important revelations, but we should hold on to our dreams and take these revelations seriously.

God warns His people today through dreams like He did in the Bible. Joseph ended up rich, but he was plunged into his arduous trek to his destiny as a result of a dream that elicited his brothers' envy (see Gen. 37:5). Because of her dream, Pilate's wife warned him of his impending decision (see Matt. 27:19). Saul bemoaned that God no longer spoke to him in dreams (see 1 Sam. 28:15), implying he'd previously been led by them. Solomon's great wisdom resulted from a dream (see 1 Kings 3:5). Daniel, Ezekiel, and Jacob proceeded on God's direction through dreams. Even Jesus' birth included dreams—wise men made travel decisions based on a warning dream about Herod, and Joseph married his bride then journeyed based on God's word from dreams (see Matt. 1–2). Like biblical dreamers, these revelations are powerful, perfect, and plentiful; we should learn how our dreams work prophetically.

Our Treasure

I take Isaiah's words seriously that before a new event occurs, we'll know (see Isa. 43:19). This means whenever something is slated to happen, even in our nation or world, God tells seers. Dreams inform us about what God wants us to know. Imagine the heartache we would have been spared if we always listened to our dreams. Even the heathen king, Nebuchadnezzar, correctly explained their importance when he noted Daniel's operation in his gift: "I know that the Spirit of the Holy God is in you, and no secret troubles you" (Dan. 4:9). No secret is withheld if we listen to these revelations. In my experience, events that come into our lives are often filtered through God by His "treasures of darkness" (Isa. 45:3). That's just what dreams are— treasures! God intimately knows His children and their futures and apprises them of what's ahead through these treasures, so nothing's a surprise. That's why when something seemingly bad happens, I look back. Did God warn me with a dream, unction, prophetic word? Did it cross my mind that I should be careful? If not, I figure He's allowing whatever's happening, so my attitude changes toward my dilemma.

Many dreams are about minor occurrences to come; but usually they're important, even about life or death. Once, I dreamed I was working in Mexico when a safety issue arose and my sister Anita died. When I asked why, someone said, "Hepatitis alarm." Often, words in dreams seem weird; but even if I don't understand, I write them down exactly as I heard them because they're important. In the morning, a Google search for that phrase revealed articles written in one language—Spanish. Those "signos de alarmas" were signs a person should heed when he/she contracts hepatitis. It said hepatitis is prevalent in border towns where the water supply is often tainted. When I called Anita, she told me her job had been sending her a few miles away to a Mexican border town. God gave two warnings—safety and disease. She heeded them. Otherwise, her fate could have been different.

Dreamers have been given God's knowledge to avoid pitfalls and grow in Him. As I said in the last chapter, Joel prophesied about dreams' importance. Then as Peter addressed the crowd at Pentecost, he quoted Joel to emphasize both their importance and common occurrences in God's scheme of today's gifts: "And it shall come to pass afterward that I will pour out My spirit on all flesh; your sons and your daughters shall prophesy, your old men shall dream dreams, your young men shall see visions" (Joel 2:28; see Acts 2:17). Holy Spirit was poured out on young and old, including night visions. I love it!

Understanding Dreams

These revelations are normally words of wisdom warning about future events. However, they also can tell about things happening now. Once, Wade and I had planned a lunch with young lady we mentored. The night before, I dreamed about a destructive situation in her life. We then knew how to pray. The next day, when I told her the message God had shown me, she opened up fully. Understanding our dreams is a process we get better at as we receive more revelations, but we must approach meanings carefully. Three elements—revelation, interpretation, and application—are all important and must be correct for that dream's message to be solid and for us to know how to act upon it. If one aspect is wrong, we might miss what God's saying; then the dream hurts rather than helps.

Revelation

The first thing to decide is if ours or another's dreams are from God. First, when we dream or others share a dream, we should pray and ask God for guidance in determining its legitimacy. When others come with a dream about us, we should proceed wisely and consider personal motivations. People can be wrong—purposely trying to mislead, attempting to manipulate, or just making a mistake. We must decide on the dream's spirituality and source. Deuteronomy 13:1-5 tells of charlatans claiming to have dreams. Jeremiah 23:25 and 32 also tell how false prophets will say "I have dreamed, I have dreamed" (verse 25) and cause others to err because they trusted the supposed dreamer. Zechariah 10:2 also talks about "false dreams." Unfortunately, as in all aspects of our lives, we must be judicious about whom we trust, even in dreaming.

However, others' dreams about us aren't the only time we should consider if the dream is from God. We should contemplate our own dream's validity. People ascertain their dream's legitimacy differently. Some say they know it's right if they remember it. If it has specific details, others know it's spiritual. Some say if it bothers them, they know it's from God (see Dan. 2:1). Others just know in their knower. If we decide the revelation is important, we must determine its source—God or satan? Some dreams seem God-sent, but actually the devil's trying to fool us. My mother once dreamed an angel said she had to let her ailing child die so she and Dad could pursue ministry. As a young Christian, Mom thought this seemed like a dream from God, but the message wasn't scriptural. She refused to accept her daughter's death, so my sister was healed. Satan is crafty and can manipulate thoughts even in dreams. By the way, when in doubt, always check the Word.

We must be led by Holy Spirit because even seemingly spiritual dreams can be caused by many things. Sometimes, "a dream comes through much activity" (Eccles. 5:3) and reflects what we're contemplating or doing in our lives. They might also be brought on by physical factors: "It shall even be as when a hungry man dreams, and look—he eats...a thirsty man dreams, and look—he drinks" (Isa. 29:8). We might dream because of external occurrences—we're cold because the covers are off, or we dream of a bell because the phone's ringing. Our joyful or despondent frame of mind can affect dreaming. We should consider that external factors influence dreams when determining validity and not act upon something we're not sure is from God. However, picking up on things around us and then dreaming can be a good thing. We may dream about being pursued by a demon because a spirit is in the room, and we're incorporating that spirit into our dreams. Then the cause of the dream—more than the dream itself—is crucial. I've awakened from dreams and perceived an evil spirit I hadn't felt while I was awake because in our sleep our spirit becomes more sensitive. That dream gives a heads up to eliminate whatever has found its way into our homes.

Write It Down

If you know the revelation is from God, you must keep it fresh in your mind in case events occur later; so just like with visions, carefully record your dreams (see Dan. 7:1). When I awaken and think I should write down a dream, I do that right then. Whenever I've lazily thought I'd surely recall it in the morning, I haven't. I keep paper in the bedside drawer and jot down enough main details to help me remember it until I can write out the entire dream. Since details are important, record everything because you may forget when you come back later; those details will give you a blueprint of God's message.

You may remember your dream for a while; but after a few months or years when the situation actually comes to pass, you may have forgotten details or even the whole dream if you didn't write it down. Job comments about how dreams are evasive: "He shall fly away like a dream, and not be found; yes, he will be chased away like a vision of the night" (Job 20:8). My dreams usually take a while to occur, so I keep mine in a notebook. When Wade and I need direction, we often go to that dreams journal to see if He already has spoken. Sometimes, we come across a forgotten dream that perfectly addresses the situation and gives amazing instruction. That couldn't happen if I didn't record them carefully.

Once, Wade and I felt led to start training ministers for people's individual needs. After a few weeks of planning, we scheduled our training. For the first training day, I went through my dreams journal to find one we could practice interpreting together. I looked through quite a few for one not too personal but with elements to make that dream's interpretation doable. I found one I'd forgotten from exactly one year before that training day, even before the individual ministry idea was conceived. It gave instructions, confirmations, and warnings for how we should proceed. Because I'd recorded it, we could continue with definite direction from God.

Interpretation

So you know that dream is from the Lord. What do you do now? That's when interpretation is important. Though sometimes I know right away what God's telling me, He rarely gives a slam-dunk interpretation because though some details are literal, usually they're symbolic. God wants to see how much you desire to know what He's saying. He hides His riches and doesn't reveal them to just anyone. Then He rewards those who seek the treasure. That's why praying again is important because "do not interpretations belong to God?" (Gen. 40:8). Even if you think you know what He's saying, often you don't understand fully, so you should seek Him.

Guard the dream's specifics and keep going back to those. Because you're dealing with pure communication between you and God, the revelation is solid even if your initial interpretation is iffy.

Yours and others' limited thoughts and experiences may incorrectly add up details, or perhaps you interpret a dream based on what you want it to say. Seek the interpretation diligently, though sometimes that interpretation won't be clear until the future like in my individual ministry dream. Dreamers aren't automatic interpreters; but with practice, analysis ability gets better. When people ask me to help them interpret, some meanings seem elementary, but not to the dreamer. When I say what it sounds like, they often act like a light just came on. That illumination inside the dreamer is what interpretation is about.

When you can interpret, people rely on you just like both Daniel and Joseph were sought out when ungodly kings had dreams they couldn't decipher. To help you discover God's meaning, find someone who's good at interpreting. My sister Suzy is amazing at unraveling a dream's layers, so talking it out with her and hearing things aloud helps the meaning jump out at me. However, rarely can one person interpret another's entire dream. Although Suzy knows me well, she doesn't know all nuances of my daily life. That's why interpreters usually look at individual elements to see how they add up to a big picture. Sometimes, as you or someone else interprets, you may start down a path that leads nowhere. If that happens, back up, look at it again, and set off another way so it makes sense.

To do that, start with resources. Everyone needs a glossary that gives universal interpretations. We've included a brief one in this book's appendix. I began compiling these symbols many years ago. When we pastored, one of our church's small groups was for those with dreaming in common. The group, which eventually became known as the Dream Team, met once a week to share dreams and help one another with interpretation. As our interpreting progressed, our list of symbols grew longer. Since then, I've added others from various sources, including mine and others' dreams. Mostly, though, I've found symbols as I've read the Bible.

Use a glossary as a starting point, but don't rely too heavily on it or any other general reference because symbols don't always mean the same thing from dream to dream. Other resources help too. Some people use a simple dictionary. Words have multiple meanings; often, one definition will say exactly what God wants to tell you. Another excellent help is a concordance, where you can look up specific dream elements and perhaps find a corresponding Scripture. Although outstanding online sources deal with symbols, be careful which site you choose. Some have a great wealth of symbols, but their publisher is new age. Though on the surface the symbols seem fine, if it's not from a Christian source, beware!

Your best asset for dream interpretation is other dreamers. However, when you share dreams, observe certain protocols. With your dream mentor, tell each detail so he/she can help fully with the interpretation. In contrast, when you're in a group, don't share your entire dream. I've been in prayer meetings where one person has told three or four dreams in minute detail. That's counterproductive for getting your interpretation because people get lost in minutiae and lose interest. Next time you're in a group when someone is telling an in-depth dream, look around. People glaze over because details don't matter to them. If the group needs to pray about the dream, tell just the bottom line—"I had a dream and think the Lord is warning us…." That's adequate to accomplish your mission of intercession.

The Symbols

With your individual interpreters, though, each detail is crucial. Interpretations are often in bits and pieces that add up. As you or another tells a dream, jotting down notes allows you to focus on key elements. Then talk out various parts. As I said, one place to start is with universal symbols. Once, when Wade and I took our young grandson Grant to see an animated movie, a firefly flew above another animal's head. When his tail flashed, Grant leaned toward me and said, "He just had an idea." That's a universal symbol even a child understood. Many symbols are consistent; examples of these are:

- vehicles = ministries
- dawn = new day
- snakes = spirits
- light bulb above the head = revelation

Consider those but realize, too, that some symbols are specifically yours. Usually, when I dream about my childhood house, God is talking about my ministry roots. However, just when I think I have symbols figured out, God mixes it up, and they mean something different.

Idioms, phrases in every language that aren't literally interpreted, are also important. For example, if you say "crack the window," native English speakers understand that expression means to open slightly rather than to break it. Idioms are often keys to a dream's meaning. You may dream you're in a bed at work, and God's telling you that you're lying down on the job. Idioms may range from "barking up the wrong tree" to "skating on thin ice," but discovering an idiom hidden away in your dream goes a long way to interpretation. I've listed a few idioms at the end of the "Dreams and Visions Symbols Glossary" in the appendix.

Consider all the dream's aspects. What feeling did you get from people, actions, or the overall dream? Were you participating? If you were just observing, where were you in the action? Dreams are usually black and white, so colors are important. Also, though dreams are often symbolic, maybe one element is literal and gives clues to the interpretation. When my daughters were in college, I had a symbolic dream with a specific warning. In one part, though, a shower curtain was in the basement. As it turned out, one roommate had just bought curtains for her basement bedroom windows—shower curtains. As you seek the interpretation, twists, turns, and dead ends may occur before you arrive at the message. Don't get frustrated and give up. Remember, God wants you to get that meaning.

Application

So you had a spiritual dream. You searched Scripture and other helps and found the interpretation. If you, like Daniel, know "The dream is certain, and its interpretation is sure" (Dan. 2:45), now what do you do? Even if you understand what God's saying but don't apply it correctly, the revelation could produce negative results. So consider many things; but first and most importantly, pray again to apply correctly the dream's message. As simple as that sounds, it's the key to finding God's heart and will. Once you know the dream's message, do everything to get victory over the situation about which you dreamed; then rest and know it's done.

The first way dreamers err is by rushing, wanting the dream to come to pass in their time, not God's. Often, a time element is in your dream. For example, if you dreamed of a child, how old was that child in the dream? How long will it be until he/she is that old? If a certain flower was blooming, when will that happen? Spring? Late summer? If people were together who usually aren't, when will that happen? I once dreamed about the church I attended, and my daughters and their friend were there. Those girls had nothing to do with my church and were rarely together because they'd all graduated from college and gone to different states. Then I realized God was telling me this event would happen at church in the fall, when those three were coming home for a wedding. It happened just that way.

As I said before, some dreams take a long time, often years, to come to pass. Like with other revelations, when you don't know the timing, just wait. However, even though the event doesn't happen immediately, that doesn't negate the dream's importance because "the vision of the evenings and the mornings which was told is true; therefore seal up the vision, for it refers to many days in the future" (Dan. 8:26). In the meantime, while you're waiting for the "many days" to pass, you "seal" it in your heart and your dreams journal. If you remember details, God's instructions will be fresh when His timing is perfect. For more than ten years, I've dreamed about our ministry, which was represented by a big, new house with lots of rooms. Elements were varied, but the message was consistent. Then, things began falling into place as He gradually put us into new ministries. God's timing for Joseph was about twenty years for his dream to come to pass because He had work to do in him to make him destiny-ready. God also had work to do in us Urbans before He could take us into our big, new house.

Reasons for Dreams

A dream's purpose may determine its application. Maybe God wants to encourage. Gideon was strengthened when he overheard a conversation at the enemy's camp about a dream foretelling Israel's victory over the Midianites (see Judg. 7:13). As I was awaiting fulfillment of the big-new-house dreams, our ministry seemed to be going backward, not forward. When I felt particularly discouraged, my mother dreamed that time had passed, and our ministry had exploded in effectiveness. Her dream said, "Just wait, Connie. It's gonna happen." Those dream promises build encouragement and faith as we hold on to God's rhema.

God also instructs through dreams. This directive says, "If you do this, I'll do this" or "This is how I want you to proceed." We give our own kids guidance for their success—education, money management, marriage choices. Here, God's Spirit hand delivers direction in His midnight express. He told Joseph how to apply Pharaoh's dream so in seven years nations would survive famine. When things looked bad for Paul in Corinth, God revealed in a night vision that he should speak and wouldn't be hurt. He trusted God and preached there for eighteen months (see Acts 18:9-11). Dreams warn of danger or bad outcome. Usually, by acting on them that situation can be avoided like when Joseph skirted danger by going into Egypt then staying in Galilee, not Judea (see Matt. 2:13-22). A dream could be an FYI, a heads up confirming God's will, revelation of a duplicitous situation, or knowledge of how to pray about a need.

Cautions!

Often, dreams have dual meanings, so you may find God telling you about both circumstances. Also, I've sometimes prayed over a dream and thought God had taken care of it, but then I dreamed it again. Dreaming something twice means "the thing is established by God, and God will shortly bring it to pass" (Gen. 41:32). Then when you dream it yet again, it's imminent and God's shouting a warning; it's important to do more than just pray and believe it's done. You should seriously seek God with intercessors to get victory over satan's plans. God warns then warns again because He wants it eradicated. Like so many other things, I've learned that lesson the hard way.

Beware. The dreamer must be grounded in the Word and in his life because some people go off on tangents. Be Spirit-led. Watch personal snares—condemnation, fear, frustration, acting too quickly. Beware of whom you trust to give revelations and how deeply you rely on those. Even the unsaved can dream spiritually. Laban, a scoundrel, had a God-given dream while pursuing Jacob (see Gen. 31:24). Abimelech, a heathen king, took Sarah as his wife; because of a spiritual dream, he knew return her because she was also Abraham's wife (see Gen. 20:3). By the way, I'm sometimes asked why people whose lives aren't right with God can still hear from Him. Just like one may receive an irrevocable trust from his grandfather, Holy Spirit's gifts are given forever (see Rom. 11:29). Despite an ungodly lifestyle, someone still may hear from God, but those revelations are often flawed because of sin or character. That's why it's important to consider not just the gifts but also the fruit of another's life.

Though people not in fellowship with God may dream accurately or even operate in other gifts, treat their revelations with caution, especially interpretations. Don't discount that message totally, though. Once, God had put on my heart that I needed to sell my tiny car and get a safer one. I'd been procrastinating; then my nephew, who didn't claim to be walking with God, called with a dream about my safety. The culmination was that a demon bragged that though I'd avoided other pitfalls, "She still has to drive." The message was clear, so I traded cars that weekend. God had repeatedly given me that message, but my nephew's dream confirmed and shouted it.

Be wary if someone seems certain of an interpretation that doesn't resound with you. Whereas Christians don't walk by feelings, when you're in the Spirit, you can trust those feelings when Holy Spirit bears witness in *your* spirit. I've known people who whipped out an interpretation quickly and authoritatively, but it wasn't accurate. Their seeming so sure of a meaning that didn't resonate with the dreamer was confusing. When Joseph interpreted for the baker then Pharaoh, they both knew that interpretation was right (see Gen. 40:16; 41:37). Once you have the basic interpretation, chew on it until details add up. Then, before you act, make sure you know the timing.

Other People

We're often asked what dreamers should do when they dream about others. My answer is succinct—you should do *something*. If you don't, how can God entrust future revelation to you? However, be led by the Lord as you consider telling dreams to another. Some are meant for you to pray about but not to share for a multitude of reasons. They may say negative things that cause offense and discouragement to the immature, or some people may become frustrated and confused because they take details literally instead of symbolically. That's why telling the bottom line is sufficient, instead of revealing details that might cloud the message. Some people are weak in faith, so the dream may cause fear and negate God's purpose.

We dreamers understand the revelation's importance, but it's often misunderstood by nondreamers or even less mature dreamers. Before Wade and I began dating, God gave me a dream about him. Though I knew his mother, I'd met Wade only once and didn't know how he and his family felt about dreams. Therefore, when I awoke, I asked God to give me another dream if He wanted me to share it. That night, I had two more. When I contacted him and shared them, as it turned out, his family *was* skeptical about dreaming—not anymore. Not only were those dreams right on, but now Wade and his family have witnessed how dreams give amazing revelations.

Sometimes you dream about a person and don't understand the dream's meaning because you aren't privy to all situations of his/her life. If you know you're supposed to tell the dream, just share and let that person come to his/her own conclusions. Use judgment, and that varies depending on the message. If you seek God, He's faithful to direct about how and when to share, how much to reveal, or even if you should tell it at all. He wants to show Himself mighty and not hurt little ones in the process.

When God gave me a warning dream that a lady who didn't believe in the gifts would suffer a stroke, I reflected about sharing it because *stroke* is a fear-inciting word. The more I sought the Lord, though, I felt led to share and pray for her. In a couple weeks, she did have a mild one. When I visited her in the hospital, she grabbed my hand and said, "You knew this would happen." Because God led me to tell her in advance, I was able to explain that because God came before and we prayed, she'd be all right. She was, and she learned about Holy Spirit's might and revelatory power.

Let God lead you so you know what He's saying; then you'll know what to do about the dream. At times you shouldn't tell the dream because it's actually not about that person. Sometimes, it's the name, personality, or job that's the key to the dream's meaning. Other elements about that person, like when he/she was in your life, may be the significance. When my youngest brother Jason was born, our church installed my dad as pastor; in many of my mother's dreams, Jason represented their pastoring. Seeking God's wisdom will always tell you what to do with your dream.

Conclusion

Wade and I are football fans, so I love this analogy comparing those who operate in the prophetic to a game. We all occupy different positions. If you're a receiver (seer), the Quarterback (Holy Spirit) wants to throw you the ball (revelation). However, if you're not paying attention, He'll still throw that ball, but He must find a different receiver. When you're bogged down with cares, sins, or activities, you're not available to hear what the Spirit has to say. That tells me if I take my gifts seriously, I should make myself available for Him. I can skip that favorite TV show, set aside my exciting novel, or pare down activities so I'm ready when He sends His message. His night visits are a sweet gift from Him that I don't want to miss.

I read something once that touched me. When Genesis 37:5 says "Joseph had a dream," that Hebrew word means "to bind firmly."[1] Joseph's dream, as with ours, became reality to which he was bound. Jack Hayford says, "'Joseph had a dream,' but perhaps we could more accurately say that the dream had Joseph."[2] Wow! When God communicates to us through dreams, we can hold on to them because they're God's promise of destiny, which is bound to us. Of all God's methods of revelation, dreams are one of the dearest forms of communication from Him to man. They're a powerful, wonderful weapon in your Holy Spirit arsenal that defeats anything satan throws your way. Being forewarned and forearmed, you can then proceed with your eyes wide open.

DISCERNMENT OF SPIRITS

Connie

When you think of the revelation gift of discernment of spirits, you automatically think of the demonic realm, but that's just part of it. As a Spirit-filled creation, you have the ability to discern both good and evil. When Elisha came by the Shunammite woman's house, she discerned he was a man of God and built him a room. Through Holy Spirit, you can perceive whether people are operating in good or bad spirits and thus know their fruit. That perception grows with exposure, and you become sensitive to the spirit realm because you sense it just as if a human were standing beside you. I've felt such distinct demonic presences I got chills and angelic presences so real I tingled. Whether you're discerning spirits around people, places, or situations, this gift is essential to spiritual growth and well-being. As a Spirit-filled believer, discernment of spirits is a very real part of the arsenal of gifts you receive.

The Demonic Realm

Our view of satan has been skewed by movies of heads spinning or women impregnated by a suave lucifer. He perpetrated that lie to keep people confused about who he is and how he works. The demonic realm is real and ugly. He originally was part of the heavenlies, but he fell; now his job is to infiltrate this earthly realm. Man has dominion over the earth, so demons look for humans through whom they can wreak havoc. They come in seemingly innocent ways but are crafty and wicked. They're dispatched to situations because they want to destroy believers physically and spiritually (see Matt. 17:15).

First Kings shows how satanic spirits work. Ahab sought counsel from his false prophets who spoke with "a lying spirit" (1 Kings 22:22). As a result of that spirit, Ahab was killed in battle. Even those with prophetic titles can be influenced by ungodly things or people, so we must discern each situation. Most tragedies happen because of evil spirits—sicknesses, catastrophes, mental illness, and others. We can defeat the enemy through the Spirit, but the key is understanding that our authority is from Jesus' sacrifice on Calvary. We aren't to fear him and his henchmen because we're overcomers, but we also can't underestimate their power. They're defeated but, in the meantime, are avidly trying to destroy us. Our job is to recognize and deal with them while realizing the spirit—not the person—needs to be attacked, uprooted, and displaced. Just because you know someone has a spirit, though, doesn't mean it's up to you to cast it out or off. The Word is clear. If a demon leaves and the host allows it back, he'll be in worse shape than before—it will come back with seven more (see Matt. 12:43-45).

Revelation of Spirits

When you minister, be aware that evil spirits can control people, activities, and circumstances. On the other hand, angels come for a wonderful purpose. Often I perceive heavenly spirits, especially as I worship. When they show up, those angels may be taking your worship to the Father, helping you war, or even taking someone home to be with Jesus. Angels are a real part of this world and dispatched for our overcoming life. As part of your gift of discernment of spirits, you can recognize both types of spirits because "the anointing which you have received from Him abides in you, and…the same anointing teaches you concerning all things, and is true, and…you will abide in Him" (1 John 2:27). Holy Spirit teaches everything from how to hear

from Him about others' needs to how to spot in which spirit someone operates. You shouldn't be afraid of either heavenly or demonic
spirits because, as this Scripture says, just as that anointing abides in
you, you also abide in Him.

If you've never experienced evil spirits, you will sometime,
and ignoring them doesn't make them any less real. Each day, we
fight a spiritual battle, so don't just take everyone and everything at
face value. You should "not believe every spirit, but test the spirits,
whether they are of God; because many false prophets have gone out
into the world" (1 John 4:1). Testing spirits extends to those you
meet daily or who profess to give words from God. How do you
test them? First, pray. Also, as people operate in their gifts, as I said
before, examine their fruit, not just their anointing and gifts. Is that
little voice in your spirit saying something isn't quite right? Are their
words aligning with *the* Word? When you can't separate truth from
lies, God's Word can cut through façades you're thrown off by. Trust
the Lord to speak to you. You can *always* trust Holy Spirit's voice
saying "uh-uh" in your ear.

Our Homes

Solomon says, "Like a flitting sparrow, like a flying swallow, so a
curse without cause shall not alight" (Prov. 26:2). Unless an open
door exists in your life, that demon can't come in. Open doors—like
sexual sin, fear, or past sin from which you haven't repented—give
legal access to your life. Abortions and former sexual sins need soul
ties broken. Also, if you've experimented with or are still dabbling
in the occult, you've allied yourself with the demonic, so you must
renounce it to close that door. Even something seemingly innocent
like Ouija boards, horoscopes, and fortune cookies bring the satanic
up close and personal. Luke calls these "spirit[s] of divination" (Acts
16:16), open doors for demons. My friend was laughing one day
about a fortuneteller who called and told her about her future. By listening, she'd allowed evil to come into her ear gate and therefore her

body and home. A few days later, she called crying because she had a terrible dream about a satanic attack on her toddler. We rebuked that spirit she'd innocently allowed in. If you ask, God will illuminate doors you've opened by past actions; then you can renounce to remove whatever it is.

Some people wonder how and where we may encounter evil spirits. They're not only in bars or hotel rooms where many have stayed; demons can also be in our own houses. Although we have godly lives, we don't know what's been done in that house that allowed a spirit to enter. We should pray over it before we move in and other times too by anointing doors, windows, and every room, then commanding unclean spirits to leave. We should also pray over any item that might allow a spirit entrance, even televisions and computers. And once is not enough. Occasionally, spirits enter even after we've anointed our houses. We might not pick up on the spirit if we've been around it a while because it not only hides but becomes a familiar spirit. As I said in the "Dreams" chapter, occasionally, I don't perceive it until I'm sleeping and it intrudes in my dream. When I awaken, I feel it distinctly.

Spirits may enter in many ways—i.e. movies or online sites, such as pornography. Also, objects used in voodoo or pagan religions associated with the demonic can have an evil presence. Once, as I prayed over a young man's house, I picked up on an evil spirit in his office where he had figurines from an island visit. Another time, the spirit was concentrated in a house's mudroom where a husband returned from his ungodly lifestyle and left his dirty clothes. In children's rooms, I've felt spirits from scary movies, witchcraft books, or seemingly innocent games with a demonic basis. Through exposure, you'll become more sensitive; and spirits' locations in the house give clues to what the spirit is, how it gained access, and how to get rid of it. Don't assume living with those won't bring consequences. They can affect your family, even years down the road.

At Church

Another place you may discern spirits is right in church. Often, people create problems because they're influenced by spirits. The Jezebel spirit manipulates and controls but usually behind the scene and closely connected with leadership. These people often volunteer regularly so they become indispensable and subsequently get their way. Every Jezebel needs an Ahab, so those spirits work in tandem. An Ahab is a leader who allows himself to be manipulated by one having a Jezebel spirit. Other spirits that can operate within a family or church are Absalom, who goes behind leaders' backs and ingratiates himself with others for his advancement. Also Korah operates in rebellion and undermines leadership.

A problem with these spirits is because they're often operating among leadership or those close to them, expelling them is difficult. Some churches have had these spirits operating so long they don't know what's normal without them. If your pastor doesn't see the problem, you should attack it with prayer and fasting. However, you need a spiritual covering. When you go on the offensive against these spirits, expect extreme satanic attacks. You may not have much support for this assignment because many don't think of spirits operating but rather attribute conflicts to controlling personalities. By the same token, people credit disputes to spirits when it's just contrary people. This is when discernment is crucial. Remember, though, this warfare is against a spirit, not a person. Those operating under these spirits' influences should be freed, not hurt.

How to Perceive

Spirits, both good and bad, are perceived in many ways. Sometimes by a person's demeanor you can discern demons, such as lust and sorrow. When you experience a bad or good feeling in places or people, trust Holy Spirit. With evil spirits, like Job, your hair will stand up on your arms, you'll think someone's watching you, or you'll just have a creepy feeling. Sometimes, a rank odor comes with the demonic, just like a sweet, beautiful smell often permeates the room when you're in the presence of heavenly beings. Sometimes you may hear sounds of angel's wings or singing, but you also can audibly hear demons. Once, a lady told me that for several days a demon had been humming a couple notes lower to songs on the radio, people on television, and conversations she had with others. As a young Christian, she operated in the gifts, and Holy Spirit revealed to her that the demon was trying to give her a nervous breakdown. She took authority, and it left. Many don't know they should command it to go, so they fall prey to the demon's assignment.

You may also actually see demons or angels. I've seen both. One foggy night, I was driving home a little too fast on a dark country road when I clearly saw a demon run and hide behind a guard rail on the east side of a bridge. I immediately prayed and slowed to a crawl. On the other side, a disabled car sat in my lane. It had no lights and was hidden in that dense fog coming from the lake. I'm sure seeing that demon saved me from crashing.

Though I've felt angels many times and have seen them with my "other eyes" often, I've witnessed them with my natural eyes rarely. Once, I was sleeping fitfully because my heart was heavy—I'd been grieving intensely because my dad was dying. I awakened abruptly when a rainbow with a tail made a slight noise as it flew in the open window. It traveled to the foot of my bed and stopped like it was protecting me. As I watched, the rainbow changed to an angel from ceiling to floor. His robes were white like a very thick mist. Such peace covered me I couldn't stay awake. That peace helped me through my terrible time.

Demonic Possession

Two levels of the demonic can plague a person—possession and oppression. With possession, a demon inhabits; with oppression one hangs around to harass or ultimately possess. Many examples occur throughout Scripture (see Mark 5:1-9). Whether a person is possessed or oppressed, as you do warfare to rid him/her of the demon you'll feel and see it rise up. The most obvious way is in the person's eyes. When you look directly at him/her, the demon squirms. Often, though, it will remain hidden until you pray. Then it tries to stop you from casting it out. I've seen intense hatred as the demon looked from inside his victim and realized I was casting him from his home. When I first saw that look, I was taken aback by the loathing, but then I realized the devil looks at us like that all the time. Demons hate the prophetic that discerns their secretive existence then casts them out.

When that occurs, more pronounced demonstrations may manifest. The voice often changes to a deeper, gravelly sound; they may spew profanities or exhibit disruptive, bizarre behavior like drooling. Sometimes, they become seductive or intimidating and say something personal. Your best response is, "Shut up and come out!" When I was young, I remember seeing A.A. Allen cast out demons, and they gave specific messages like whom they would indwell next. They also can give clues about how they came to occupy, like through abuse as a child. When you know that, you can pray more effectively. As a Spirit-filled believer, you have authority, but I don't believe you should be a "demon chaser" and purposely seek to cast them out. Satan likes attention, so don't go out of your way to acknowledge him. When the time comes, though, just do it and "submit to God. Resist the devil and he will flee from you" (James 4:7). Remember the first part. We must submit to and be in partnership with God.

Knowing the Spirit

Just like angels have ranks and certain heavenly jobs, demons have a hierarchy and specific responsibilities (see Matt. 17:21). Some demons are assigned for one purpose—calamity. Through previous exposure, you can recognize that demon and discern its job. My mom experienced that when I was young, and I encountered a specific spirit multiple times as an adult. I had a distinct feeling something bad was going to happen one day after work. I was sitting halfway down a hill in an after-school traffic jam when a distracted teenager rammed into the back of my car. A few months later I felt that same spirit as a semi barreled up behind me on the highway. Remembering Mom's stories, I prayed during the trip, knowing his crashing into me would certainly mean my death in that small car. Arriving safely in town, I turned while the truck drove on. Sighing in relief, I sat a block away at a stoplight and awaited my turn when another car drove up and rear-ended me. I perceived that spirit well enough to pray against being hit by the truck but didn't call protection from all accidents. We learn.

Conclusion

Spiritual discernment, both good and bad, is a fact of Holy Spirit life. This gift allows you to determine what's going on in the spiritual realm, perceive others' motives, and see whether they're operating from their flesh rather than their spirit (see Gal. 5:19-21). It lets you detect which spirit one is influenced by to know how to relate to that person or to help him/her get delivered from oppression or possession. This aspect of our gifts is deep, difficult, and sometimes downright messy, but it's necessary. Each Spirit-filled believer is equipped to discern spirits but must remember one important thing—love. That's a message you'll hear often in this book. Paul reminds us that no matter how mature we are in faith and gifts, if we forget to love, nothing else matters (see 1 Cor. 13:2). A love stance says we're warring against a spirit, not a person, and nothing evil can stand with Jesus' love.

Discerning the spirit in which a person operates is crucial—from leaders in a church, to that new man who asked you for a date, to that person who wants you to invest in his amazing financial plan, to that seemingly prophetic person who just gave you a word. If you trust that your Father can show you spirits that so adeptly hide, you'll make God-ordained choices and thus have peace. Just like you give your family to God's care, believe He'll let you know what you need to perceive. Trusting Him to reveal what spirit a person comes in will make a discernible difference in your life.

ONE TO GROW ON: MOSES' TABERNACLE

Wade

Promotion within military ranks doesn't happen overnight. A combination of training and practical experience is required to grow in effectiveness, authority, and rank. No one in the military would take a raw recruit and put a powerful weapon in his hands until he's trained and demonstrated through practical experience the required degree of expertise in its operation. That same inexperienced recruit would also never be given authority to command others, particularly in combat. This concept of training and practical experience with Holy Spirit's arsenal applies to development as spiritual warriors. Spiritual training and experience begin by renewing our minds to prove God's will on earth (see Rom. 12:1-2). The renewing of our minds is a continuous process of being conformed to Christ and understanding the finished work of Lord Jesus Christ—Holy Spirit's life through us. This combination of His Word and practical experience is necessary to grow in spiritual authority and power.

The Bible demonstrates the concept of progression in several places. Ezekiel's river of God flowed from God's throne, first ankle deep, then knee deep, waist deep, and finally waters to swim in (see Ezek. 47: 1-12). Also, the ten gates in Nehemiah 3 describe our Christian walk as we grow toward our destiny, as Connie describes in her book *God's Plan for Our Success Nehemiah's Way*. Even prophets' and patriarchs' lives show a progression as they experienced God's redemptive character. As with everything about our God-walk, ability to receive Holy Spirit's revelation and operate in His power is a maturing process.

Moses' tabernacle is an excellent example of maturing in the gifts. Moses' tabernacle, also known as the Tabernacle in the Wilderness, had three sections—the Outer Court, Holy Place, and Holy of Holies (see Exod. 25–31). This tabernacle is a type of progression from our salvation experience to intercession in partnership with Holy Spirit. Through the tabernacle, we can better understand our Holy Spirit journey.

Outer Court

The brazen altar was the first station in the Outer Court. Here, sacrifices and offerings were made by the Levites. The brazen altar is a type of Calvary, where the final sacrifice of the Lamb of God was made for sin. The bronze laver represents "washing of water by the Word" (Eph. 5:26), where renewing the mind begins (see Rom. 12:1-2). The Outer Court is symbolic of the beginning of our walk with God. Open to natural elements, it symbolizes the new believer's carnal nature. Justification, salvation of our spirit-man, occurs here as we learn to become God's dwelling place.

In the Outer Court, we're delivered from sin's power and begin the renewing process of our minds at the bronze laver, symbolizing God's Word. The renewed mind begins with comprehension of this "new creation" lifestyle (see 2 Cor. 5:17). Praise is our response to newfound freedom received at the cross. Today, most of the church lives in an Outer Court environment, going no deeper than their justification experience. Justification occurs in our spirit man and qualifies us for equipping through Holy Spirit.

Holy Place

The Holy Place represents activation (baptism) of Holy Spirit in a believer's life. The golden lampstand filled with olive oil burned continually and provided illumination, symbolic of the Spirit's revelation. The table of showbread was constructed of acacia wood overlaid with gold, simultaneously representing humanity and divinity. Upon the table were twelve (number of government) loaves of bread—symbolic of Lord Jesus Christ, all man yet all God, "the firstborn among many brethren" (Rom. 8:29). Isaiah perfectly describes the table of showbread's symbolism of Jesus: "For unto us a Child is born, unto us a Son is given; and the government will be upon His shoulder" (Isa. 9:6). The final article in the Holy Place was the golden altar of incense, containing sweet spices—stacte, onycha, galbanum, and frankincense of equal amounts (see Exod. 30:34).

As the priest brought a coal from the brazen altar and lit sweet spices, the smoke and savory fragrance—representing worship—filled the entire enclosure. Both the lampstand and altar were fashioned of pure gold, representing God. Worship is authored, initiated, and performed by Holy Spirit living within us. Jesus explained Holy Spirit's role in true worship:

> But the hour is coming, and now is, when true worshipers will worship the Father in spirit [pneuma, meaning Holy Spirit] and truth; for the Father is seeking such to worship Him. God is Spirit, and those who worship Him must worship in spirit and truth (John 4:23-24).

The Holy Place is symbolic of believers becoming *equipped* by Holy Spirit for ministry. Here, the gifts' operations are discovered and utilized. However, many stop their progression in Christ here. Some teach that the Holy Place is a believer's consummate experience this side of heaven, and we must wait for the future to experience more of God than having gifts in operation. For these folks, the Holy Place has become a false finish line as they stop short of pursuing more of His presence and purpose. As in the Outer Court, the Holy Place is where flesh is still alive, yet where the Spirit also comes alive within believers. It often brings inner frustration, knowing there must be more of His presence to experience. The Holy Place is where worship becomes vital in preparing believers for the next level of progression in their journey in Christ, for worship is the precursor to entering God's presence in the Holy of Holies.

Holy of Holies

The Holy of Holies was a four-square enclosure containing the Ark of the Covenant with the mercy seat. On the mercy seat dwelt the shekinah, glory of God. Only once each year (Great Day of Atonement), the high priest was allowed to enter the Holy of Holies and approach the ark to sprinkle the blood of sacrifice on the mercy seat to atone for the nation's sins. The Holy of Holies represents God's presence—the glory zone, from which we're to minister Holy Spirit's gifts in intercession as "kings and priests" (Rev. 1:6).

So man could enter God's presence, the Old Covenant required three levels of separation in the tabernacle. Because of the finished work of Jesus Christ, separation no longer exists, for He dwells within us by His Spirit. Paul wrote, "Do you not know that you are the temple of God and that the Spirit of God dwells in you?" (1 Cor. 3:16). Paul describes our bodies as the New Covenant Holy of Holies, where God's glory dwells. Awesome! We're God's Holy of Holies created in the Spirit to intercede and minister the gifts. The Outer Court is where we're *qualified* to be "partakers of the divine nature" (2 Pet. 1:4) as we receive Holy Spirit. The Holy Place is where we're *equipped* by activation through baptism of Holy Spirit and the operation in Holy Spirit's empowerments. We're ushered into the Holy of Holies by the Spirit through *worship*. In God's presence, we leave the cursed environment of time and space behind, entering the glory zone.

Here, we assume our positions in Christ, ministering from the mercy seat. We have clarity of a new perspective (vision) from which we clearly view past, present, and future. From the mercy seat, our ministry becomes the "spirit of prophecy" (Rev. 19:10) as we speak what we hear Holy Spirit saying and act out what we see the Spirit doing. Prophetic actions create instantaneous manifestations of kingdom reality. No more hit-and-miss ministry within the Holy Place. No more warring against a conquered foe and trying to work up faith to stand in victory. From the Holy of Holies, we minister from a position of rest, peace, and Love Himself. This is the ministry for which we were created; this is God's will for us. This is truly being positioned in Christ.

From the Holy of Holies, Father responds with signs and wonders as encouragement to go deeper in Him. Manifestations of gold dust, manna, weightiness (*kabod*), gold fillings and crowns, gold teeth, falling feathers, jewels appearing from nowhere, angelic visitations, instantaneous miracles, and healings are a few ways God's glory responds to those pursuing His presence and ministering from His glory. From God's presence, natural time and space limitations cease to exist, and instantaneous manifestations of healings and working of miracles occur. This is our place of ministry, dispersing the knowledge of the Lord's convincing splendor throughout the earth (see Hab. 2:14). Once you've experienced this, you become divinely addicted and require more of His presence. Through dependency on Him, we experience His power.

Conclusion

As you continue through this book, Connie and I hope you'll desire this progression into the glory zone of His presence. Jesus Christ is the Doorway into this Spirit-filled, glory-filled lifestyle, allowing you to minister with your gifts from the glory zone. Oh, how the church needs an outbreak of His presence to spread and consume our nation. This will happen only as you and I carry Holy Spirit's reality and God's presence from the Holy of Holies into our places of worship and into the city streets in our everyday lives.

Part II

SPEAKING GIFTS

SPEAKING GIFTS

Wade

In the military, major strategic combat operations begin with air war where enemy headquarters, strongholds, lines of communication, and supply caches are targeted for destruction and disruption. Smart bombs are released to inflict maximum damage to the enemy and his ability to carry out his operations. In spiritual warfare, we're often aware of the enemy's secrets through divine revelation. Then after we receive divine communication, we go one step further to actually speak God's truth into existence and negate the enemy's plans. Those words are our ammunition in battle. God honors His prophets' words and doesn't let them fall to the ground without accomplishing their intended mission. The speaking gifts are like bombs—they hit the target to destroy the enemy.

Those words are speaking gifts—tongues, interpretation of tongues, and prophecy—and are Holy Spirit-inspired utterances given to destroy the enemy and build up the church. These pronouncements are issued through words containing revelation as received and processed through a believer speaking from Holy Spirit's revelation. These Spirit-inspired words serve to represent the Father's heart of love for His people. His rhema spoken through believers in partnership with Holy Spirit is full of power and carries the force of faith with potential to manifest God's will. Those operating in speaking gifts not only call forth God's words but demonstrate His heart through the manner and timing of how the word is delivered. Speaking gifts carry Holy Spirit's anointing similar to how laying on of hands releases power into people's lives.

Creative Words

What's a word? It's the spoken expression of one's heart. Consider:

> *In the beginning was the Word, and the Word was with God, and the Word was God. He was in the beginning with God. All things were made through Him, and without Him nothing was made that was made. In Him was life, and the life was the light of men. And the light shines in the darkness, and the darkness did not comprehend it. ...And the Word became flesh and dwelt among us, and we beheld His glory, the glory as of the only begotten of the Father, full of grace* (John 1:1-5,14).

Jesus Christ, the Word, was the fullest expression of Father's heart of love for His creations. Jesus was His Father's voice, speaking, teaching, and demonstrating Father's love in the midst of a cursed environment. Hebrews 1:1-4 explains that God upholds all things through His Word, Jesus Christ. Paul explained that those led by the Spirit are God's children, heirs and joint heirs with Jesus Christ (see Rom. 8:17), and Jesus was the firstborn among many brethren. This implies that others who are filled with Holy Spirit have God's creative ability to speak kingdom reality into existence (see Rom. 8:29). Just as the Word (*logos*), Jesus Christ, created all things, so speaking gifts have creative power to bring Kingdom manifestations. Holy Spirit-inspired spoken words are incorruptible seeds having potential to produce harvests of righteousness and expand God's Kingdom. These spoken words carry God's truth and light to illuminate darkness.

Our Words

Words are powerful! As we examine the power of natural words, we gain a deeper appreciation of the power of the speaking gifts. A cursory examination of Scripture reveals the power of words. We're snared by our words (see Prov. 6:2), death and life are in the power of the tongue (see Prov. 18:21), we're delivered by our words (see Prov. 21:23), and we're either justified or condemned by our words (see Matt. 12:34-37).

Each of these Scriptures is about our everyday words—pretty sobering, isn't it? When we understand our tongues are attached to our hearts (see Matt. 12:34), we should certainly become more cognizant of what we allow into our spirits through what we see, hear, and meditate on. Our words are so powerful we tend to follow them. Another way of saying this is that we prophesy our own pathways and others' as well by words we speak. Believers complain about why God's covenant promises aren't working in their lives when they continually violate the kingdom principle of seedtime and harvest by planting destructive seed (their words) for future harvest (see Gen. 8:22). Through careless speaking, they unknowingly curse their own vineyards. We reap what we sow! If we truly want to change our lives, modifying what goes into our hearts must be a priority. Whatever's in the heart will eventually come out the mouth as words; then they act as nails constructing our futures. Knowing the force of natural words, consider the power contained in Holy Spirit's speaking gift.

Conclusion

When spoken forth, Holy Spirit-inspired pronouncements contain heaven's power to create Kingdom manifestations. Holy Spirit's revelation (rhema) causes faith to be initiated (see Rom. 10:17); so when we speak forth God's words, we can expect to reap His results. Faith fuels these speaking gifts so they're perfect in timing and content to bring about God's will. Words carry spiritual substance of faith or fear, going out and always returning, bringing back their payload. Isaiah says, "So shall My word be that goes forth from My mouth; it shall not return to Me void, but it shall accomplish what I please, and it shall prosper in the thing for which I sent it" (Isa. 55:11).

God's word goes out as proceeds of His heart. Creative power is in His word! The speaking gifts are one of the purest forms of partnership with Holy Spirit. They carry tremendous power to influence the present and future. As we use tongues, interpretation, and prophecy, we're charged with speaking the Father's heart using His words and employing His own language. With this power comes not just authority but also responsibility to speak with discretion and integrity.

TONGUES, INTERPRETATION, AND PRAYING IN HOLY SPIRIT

Connie

S peaking in tongues is a rallying point for many. Some hate it. Some love it. Some condemn it; some can't imagine their lives without it. Of all Holy Spirit's weapons, none causes as much controversy as this gift. Why? People don't understand it, so they dismiss or ridicule it. Some say it was for one night only, but that's a gross scriptural misinterpretation, just as with everything biblical that's ignored to suit a particular doctrine. Paul said, "Do not forbid to speak with tongues" (1 Cor. 14:39) because he understood what that gift meant in believers' lives. He knew, though, even as this amazing phenomenon was becoming widespread, controversy would erupt. In First Corinthians 14:21, Paul quotes the prophecy:

> *For with stammering lips and another tongue He will speak to this people, to whom He said, "This is the rest with which You may cause the weary to rest," and, "This is the refreshing"; yet they would not hear* (Isaiah 28:11-12).

This word is chilling. Around eight hundred years before tongues came in that Upper Room,[1] the prophet Isaiah had clearly foretold this phenomenon and others' reactions. He described it perfectly—"stammering lips and another tongue." He called it a message through which God "will speak to this people." He saw it would bring great benefits to the user as it would "cause the weary to rest [and bring] refreshing." Yet the sad part of Isaiah's prophesy describes a majority of the church world because "they would not hear." God's plan from the beginning was for His Son not only to die for our sins but also to usher in Holy Spirit, including tongues. Most Christians neglect this amazing gift, which even Isaiah touted. Tongues aren't to be ignored or belittled but are alive today for an enormous purpose.

Day of Pentecost

When disciples gathered in one accord in the Upper Room, an amazing phenomenon occurred. A heavenly sound like a "rushing mighty wind" filled the house, and fire-like tongues sat upon each of them (Acts 2:2-3). Then "they were all filled with the Holy Spirit and began to speak with other tongues, as the Spirit gave them utterance" (Acts 2:4). This came as evidence of their infilling of the Holy Spirit whom Jesus had promised. That night, tongues spoken were languages identifiable to those around; and as each spoke in tongues, others miraculously heard in their own languages.

Many detractors say this is one reason that speaking in tongues isn't for today because usually we don't speak in established languages. That's true; but though we usually don't know what Holy Spirit's saying, people even today understand tongues in their own languages. My mother, for example, went into Mexico to do missionary work on many occasions. Several times, she gave messages in tongues and was amazed at the number who responded. Later, they complimented her on her perfect use of Spanish. The irony was that my mother's limited high school Spanish was a family joke, but Holy Spirit knew that language perfectly.

When she and my sister Becky went to a service at an Arizona Indian reservation, they heard an amazing story about that phenomenon of speaking established languages in tongues. Joe, an older man, testified that he'd been a drunk, shiftless and purposeless. One night, he staggered into a service where a visiting minister was preaching.

As he looked at Joe, he thought he'd change his sermon to a salvation message for this obviously lost soul. He preached with all his heart. When he gave the altar call, Joe ran forward, crying so hard his body shook as he repented. After his sobbing subsided, the preacher put his arm around Joe and welcomed him into Jesus' family.

"What part of that sermon touched your heart, Joe?" he asked tenderly.

"Nothin'," Joe bluntly answered. "Matter a fact, it was obvious you was preachin' to me, so I 'most left. But sumpin' made me stay." While he looked into the confused preacher's face, he explained. "I was raised by my grandma. Right before ya gave that call, a young woman down front stood and said sumpin' in another language. Don't know how she knew, but it was my grandma's tongue. I knew God was talkin' jus' ta me, and I couldn't wait ta answer." He explained that her speaking the dialect was a miracle itself. It had been used far away among earlier generations and had died out as another replaced it. The girl who'd spoken in tongues was a long distance from his grandmother's tribe and way too young to have ever heard it. Her message in a tongue unknown to her had done what a polished speaker could not. Holy Spirit knew exactly how to woo Joe.

Tongues and Prophecy

In the Upper Room and today also, speaking in other tongues is the initial sign of Holy Spirit's entrance into believers' lives (see Acts 2:1-4; 19:1-6). Just as the message comes by way of divine inspiration, so does the interpretation. Both are authored by Holy Spirit, partnered with a believer, and contain power in their purpose. As Paul laid his hands on disciples, they received tongues and prophesied (see Acts 19:6). As he progressed in the gifts, he understood that though he thanked "God [that he spoke] with tongues more than you all" (1 Cor. 14:18), when there's something new and controversial, guidelines should be established. Thus, in First Corinthians 14, he provides protocols for messages in tongues given in an assembly.

Many leaders shy away from tongues because newcomers as well as the unsaved could be alienated, offended, or confused by Holy Spirit utterances. Always staying aware of the unsaved (see 1 Cor. 14:23), prophets should follow this order and keep those tender ones in their hearts. Though that shouldn't make us in any way discount tongues, we should keep that in mind and remember Paul's words:

> *If you bless with the spirit, how will he who occupies the place of the uninformed say "Amen" at your giving of thanks, since he does not understand what you say? For you indeed give thanks well, but the other is not edified* (1 Corinthians 14:16-17).

Amen! When people unfamiliar with tongues attend a service, they often become confused. Speaking in tongues too much in that service can perplex visitors enough they become turned off and may never again seek Jesus or deeper things of the Spirit. However, if Holy Spirit leads, it can be a sign to unbelievers, such as with spectators in the Upper Room. Holy Spirit provides gifts for an overcoming lifestyle. He's also in the salvation business; so He knows what it takes to draw people—healings, tongues, prophecies, or antiquated Indian dialects. Jesus came for the lost, so we should do what will draw them. Our part is to obey when Holy Spirit tells us how to proceed because He knows each situation.

Prophecy, another tool to draw the lost, comes in many forms, and one is in conjunction with tongues—a message in tongues + interpretation = prophecy. Paul, who wasn't in the Upper Room but spoke in tongues, addressed detractors when he said, "I wish you all spoke with tongues" (1 Cor. 14:5). He cherished all Holy Spirit's gifts and urged us to "desire spiritual gifts, but especially that you may prophesy" (1 Cor. 14:1). Paul wanted everyone to speak in tongues and to prophesy, but he also knew that the nature of those gifts made establishing guidelines necessary. He understood that too many unknown messages could be confusing, so he said tongues should be limited in a service (two or three) and to give them only when someone could interpret because others, not just the giver, profit by that revelation (see 1 Cor. 14:27, 6). He also said that though inter-pretation can come through anyone as Holy Spirit leads, those who give a message in tongues should pray to interpret (see 1 Cor. 14:13), or they're missing part of tongues' advantage. Despite controversy and extensive biblical guidelines, don't neglect this powerful weapon.

Prayer Language

Paul's instructions for when someone gives a message in tongues to others are clear and necessary. However, tongues leading to an interpretation are just one way Spirit-filled believers utilize that gift. Another important aspect exists, which many churches misunderstand. I've heard critics say that because no interpretation came when someone spoke in tongues, it wasn't of God because the Bible says an interpretation should follow. That's true if the tongues are meant to be interpreted. However, that's just one type in our Holy Spirit arsenal. First Corinthians 12:10 lists various gifts plus "different kinds of tongues" as manifestations of Holy Spirit. Plural. Paul knew a distinction existed between types of tongues—those which accompanied prophesy versus tongues as prayer language. When he said he wished everyone spoke in tongues, he didn't mean just in an assembly. Prayer language isn't when we get a message to share with others but rather when we pray in Holy Spirit. Both involve speaking in tongues, but each purpose is different. Prayer language is an intercessory gift and a powerful ministry weapon.

Paul tells us, "He who speaks in [an unknown] tongue does not speak to men but to God, for no one understands him; however, in the spirit he speaks mysteries" (1 Cor. 14:2). He's saying that at times we're not speaking in tongues for men to hear an accompanying message but rather only for God. When we speak in tongues in prophetic situations, men hear that. While prophecy is for others, tongues are for the individual (see 1 Cor. 14:3-4), our personal language between Him and us. Paul says in his personal life, he prays and sings in the Spirit because in that instance he's not charged with others needing to understand (see 1 Cor. 14:15). Most of the time, *we* won't even understand what we're praying. Oh, and like Paul, singing in the Spirit brings power into a situation!

Even during prayer time, satan hears our words, which can open the door for attacks as we speak doom instead of destiny. If he hears what we say, he can formulate a battle plan against us. However, only the Spirit knows what our prayer language is saying. The enemy's deceit is powerless because he doesn't understand its meaning and can't set traps to keep God's pure word from going forth and accomplishing its purpose. He knows our prayer language's power but has no defense against it as it releases God's word into circumstances. Therefore, he often uses other believers as henchmen to ridicule, condemn, and say tongues are from the devil.

A Christian's goal is to understand the "hope of His calling...the riches of the glory...and the working of His mighty power" (Eph. 1:18-19). If we know Holy Spirit's power comes by breaking through barriers in our prayer life, we overcome. When we pray in the Spirit, we aren't hindered by our own lack of faith as we speak words for something seemingly impossible. Instead, we use His words spoken through Holy Spirit to the Father. Without the powerful gift of tongues, we operate in ignorance, stay bound, and lose a great weapon.

When We Don't Know How

Tongues as a prayer language are an amazing tool when you feel dry and like your prayers are going nowhere. Holy Spirit can say those words you're having trouble saying yourself. When you know something's wrong but you don't know what it is, Holy Spirit takes over. This is a wonderful aspect of prayer language because often you don't "know what [you] should pray for as [you] ought, but the Spirit Himself makes intercession for [you] with groanings which cannot be uttered" (Rom. 8:26). This Scripture labels tongues as "groanings" you can't say on your own. When your infant can't describe his dire need, the Spirit knows. When your body's ill and doctors can't find what's wrong, Holy Spirit knows. When your son's deployed overseas too far for you to see what's happening, but during the night you awaken and need to pray, the Spirit knows. You don't always have wisdom even if you operate fluently your gifts, but Holy Spirit does.

Understanding this use of tongues changed my family's lives many times. Once, our church had scheduled a trip to an amusement park. The week before, we were excited, but something happened that made me know I should get hold of God. Each night, Jill cried out in her sleep, "Mimi!" She'd never called me that before, and her obvious distress disturbed me. Since my divorce, we'd dealt with many issues I'd shared with Holy Spirit, but this was another one too big for me. That week, because I didn't know how to pray, I relied on my prayer language. By the weekend, I felt peace but still had no idea what I'd been praying for.

I found out on Saturday. The day had been long; my sister Lynda and I welcomed the chance to sit while our kids took one last ride on the kiddie roller coaster. We saw the accident happening but were helpless to do anything when the car coming into the station rammed into the one our daughters occupied. EMS was called; many kids, looking helpless inside neck braces, were strapped to stretchers. Parents and children loaded into ambulances for the ride to the hospital. I tried unsuccessfully to talk the driver into my sitting in the back with my frightened girls, crying uncontrollably. I finally climbed into the ambulance's front seat.

As I shut the door, I called to the back, "Girls, I'm here!"

When she heard my voice, Jill twisted as much as her restraints would allow and reached toward me. "Mimi!" she cried. I got chills. Before the attendant at that amusement park had left his post, God knew all about it. I'd prayed all week and still didn't know the problem, but I knew the solution. Holy Spirit. When I heard Jill's cry, I knew everything would be okay. It was. Other children were hurt in varying degrees, but my kids were fine because Holy Spirit interceded for this yet-to-happen event. So often, I'm not smart enough to know words to say, so Holy Spirit says them for me. "For if I pray in a tongue, my spirit prays, [although] my understanding is unfruitful" (1 Cor. 14:14). My understanding is *limited*; His is *limitless*. He had our backs that day and many others because He's given us a language from Someone who knows how, when, and what to pray.

Purpose of Praying in Tongues

That's not the only reason for our personal tongues, though. Many Spirit-filled believers speak in tongues but don't understand its importance. They suffer unnecessarily—depression, sickness, disease, poverty, hopelessness—when tongues could open the door to heaven's resources. Satan's wiles can't invade lives when we understand and exercise this gift. As mentioned earlier, our lack of faith can't impede the power of God's Word from going forth and working out His plans.

So what does praying in the Spirit do? It builds our faith and edifies ourselves (see Jude 20). It's the key that releases God's wisdom in a mystery, unlocks heaven's resources, and allows access to other gifts (see 1 Cor. 2:7-11). Praying in the Spirit activates spiritual anointing, allows our eyes to see everything God has for us, and causes us to give thanks well to fulfill our purpose of worshiping God (see Eph. 1:18; 1 Cor. 14:17). We can pray effectively because "He who searches the hearts knows what the mind of the Spirit is, because He makes intercession for the saints according to the will of God" (Rom. 8:27). How do we intercede? Let Him do it for us, through us. That's His job and ours—together.

One Accord

Finally, praying in tongues reverses the confusion of languages at Babel. Wow! Tongues and prayer in Holy Spirit are the restoration of God's original purpose. Remember how people in Babel decided to build a tall tower to reach the heavens and bring themselves, not God, glory (see Gen. 11:6-9)? He scattered them by changing their language from one to many because "indeed the people are one and they all have one language—now nothing that they propose to do will be withheld from them" (Gen. 11:6). God confused languages to keep them from accomplishing too much, but now He's again given a common language—tongues. What's possible if we pray through this single language?

The confused languages stopped the wicked plans for the tower and scattered men as they gathered into nations based on languages. This Holy Spirit language restores our ability to do anything through this tongue we all can access. Zephaniah prophesied about this language: "For then I will restore to the peoples a pure language, that they all may call on the name of the Lord, to serve Him with one accord" (Zeph. 3:9). "One accord," the very phrase used when Holy Spirit was given and tongues were spoken in that Upper Room. It brings the Body of Christ back to one pure, heavenly language! Nothing can be kept from us as we go forth in unity, praying in the Spirit. God Himself said, "Now nothing [we] propose to do will be withheld from [us]." Can you get *that* promise into your spirit?

Conclusion

Yes, speaking in tongues is controversial. Yes, some think it's weird. No, in ourselves we don't understand what we're saying. Yes, some people make fun, but no worry. Even at the first anointed-tongues service, people mocked them, saying they were drunk (see Acts 2:13). Those who ridicule don't know the potential of this powerful weapon. No matter what others' perceptions are, praying in the Spirit, tongues, is one of the most powerful spiritual weapons a believer can wield against the enemy. Satan has no defense, other than trying to stop tongues from being spoken in homes and churches. We can push through, though. How? I think you know that answer!

PROPHECY

Wade

In combat, leaders' orders must be immediately communicated through the chain of command and promptly carried out. Similarly, prophecy is divine communication providing direction, confirmation, and prescribed action in spiritual warfare to break through enemy strongholds. I liken prophecy to an armored unit led by heavy tanks employed to demolish enemy strongholds as they swiftly roll through enemy defensive positions. Prophecy is an element of spiritual breakthrough anointing as Holy Spirit authors supernatural utterances filled with His power, activating angelic activity to produce miraculous results.

New Testament Prophecy

Prophecy is God's revelatory power released through the spoken word authored by Holy Spirit. Prophecy is for believers, not the unsaved (see 1 Cor. 14:22), and is for edification, exhortation, and comfort of others (see 1 Cor. 14:3). Paul explained that New Covenant prophecy is to be judged (see 1 Cor. 14:29). Under the Old Covenant, a prophet spoke with 100 percent Holy Spirit inspiration or 100 percent from flesh. The penalty for a lying prophet was stoning to death for misrepresenting God. New Covenant prophecy differs from the Old. Under the New Covenant, prophecy is to be judged as to what's of Holy Spirit or of flesh or, more practically, what percentage of that message should be discarded. When a prophecy is spoken, leadership should ensure that those receiving the message aren't misled by an overzealous speaker who either has impure motives or can't distinguish his/her own thoughts from Holy Spirit's.

Just as with other gifts, those operating in prophecy need to mature, much like learning to ride a bicycle. You need someone seasoned to steady and mentor you into understanding how Holy Spirit flows until you're balanced and can go by yourself. New Covenant prophecy, in my opinion, should no longer be, "Thus saith the Lord." That was the case in the Old Covenant; in the New, it's more like, "This is what the Lord and I have to say." Prophecy can be relayed in normal, everyday language. In my experience, prophecy isn't just for church gatherings; it's also relevant one on one over coffee outside the church building. The more mature you become, the less of you shows through in prophecy.

Those speaking a word represent God, and those prophesying are declaring that God by Holy Spirit is speaking through them. Therefore, when we prophesy, integrity requires us to relate the level or degree of divine revelation we received. A "thus saith the Lord" proclamation when the word wasn't strong may be misleading and cause hearers to believe the revelation was deeper and more authoritative than it actually was. At times, the message from God is intense and prophecy nearly bursts forth, but also quiet times come when we receive only an impression. When that happens, I might say, "Holy Spirit just impressed me with…. Does that apply to anyone?"

To Come to Fruition

The Lord is a God of order, so He loves His established protocol. If we follow that procedure, confusion won't occur from prophecy. When believers follow Holy Spirit's guidance in speaking forth His revelation as a prophetic utterance, divine power to influence lives is released. When His order is violated, spiritual damage can result. Used judiciously, prophecy is a powerful gift releasing faith's might through the spoken word. Personal prophecy should be confirmed in other ways by Holy Spirit then acted on in faith by making preparation (equipping process) for promised advancement. This requires a journey of faith and equipping over a mountain range of testing and transformation of one's character to reach the destination. Most prophecy today doesn't reveal required tests and journeys to that destination where manifestation will occur. We "see through a glass darkly" and "know in part" only what Holy Spirit reveals (1 Cor. 13:12). Those receiving words and prophesying rarely "see" the whole context, most often only a brief glimpse.

Many believers have received past prophetic words that have never manifested because New Covenant personal prophecy is conditional. Prophecy is a divine seed of possibility the Spirit releases, and its coming to pass depends upon the individual acting on it. I've seen immature believers receive elaborate prophecies from equally immature speakers. They had a future snapshot revelation from God then spoke a prophecy with a false impression of imminent results, ready to fall into hearers' laps. A prophetic word is actually a potential possibility. The revelation behind the prophecy rarely shows the entire video of where one is today and the journey to get to what the snapshot revealed. Of course, when the prophecy doesn't happen right away, many accuse the person who gave the word of being a false prophet and God for holding back His promise. Neither is the case!

Ministry Ready

All prophecy is through faith, working by love (see Gal. 5:6), the divine motivator behind all gifts. Prophecy is the direct representation of God's heart of love toward His people. They don't need to hear how far they've fallen or how bad they are; they need life ministered to heal hurts and restore brokenness. Love and humility are trademarks of prophetic character. Repentance is the key to maintaining purity of motives and actions. Because prophecy is a mix of Holy Spirit and us, we must keep short accounts with God and others. Part of our love for the Lord and our brothers is our looking inwardly to keep our hearts pure.

We can't minister what we don't have (Holy Spirit), but we'll impart what we do have (sin). That's why everyone should assess his/her life. Whatever latent sin lies within us will inevitably be imparted to others. Leviticus 21:16-23 provides symbolism of spiritual defects to be eliminated. God spoke to Moses concerning any of Aaron's descendants who would have physical defects that would prohibit them from ministering before God. Each physical defect has spiritual symbolism—lack of vision, sin in our walk, no spiritual balance, inability to carry a spiritual load (intercession), grasshopper mentality, unhealed wounds turned to bitterness, timidity, and lack of fertility and boldness. These spiritual defects are debilitating and must be eliminated in ministers.

Jesus spoke about improper motivations (see Matt. 7:21-23). Even though people prophesy, operate in deliverance, and participate in signs and wonders in His name, Jesus said He doesn't know them because they "practice lawlessness" (Matt. 7:23). In the Kingdom economy, improper motivation equals lawlessness. Paul wrote: "Let no corrupt word proceed out of your mouth, but what is good for necessary edification, that it may impart grace to the hearers. And do not grieve the Holy Spirit of God, by whom you were sealed for the day of redemption" (Eph. 4:29-30). Character flaws grieve Holy Spirit and taint our ministry to others.

Saul's a great example of attitudes that could result in tainted prophecies. At one point with Samuel, Saul had legitimately been used of God to prophesy with sons of the prophets (see 1 Sam. 10:11). Then after he disobeyed God and Samuel anointed David in his place, people exalted David's war record above Saul's (see 1 Sam. 18:7). Saul became angry, displeased, and suspicious "from that day forward" (1 Sam. 18:8-9). Basically, he envied David. Although in the past David's worship had calmed Saul's distressing spirit, after envy filled his heart, worse spirits came upon him.

One day as David attempted to calm the spirit, Saul began to prophesy (see 1 Sam. 18:10). On face value, that seems to be a good thing; but not only was he prophesying from the evil spirit's influence, he also held a spear in his hand and planned to kill David. He actually tried twice while David was with him (see 1 Sam. 18:11). How could his prophecy be legitimate when he had anger, envy, hatred, suspicion, and murder in his heart? Prophecy, even a hard word, should reflect God's heart of love. Our words will speak what's in our hearts (see Matt. 12:34); so when evil is present, prophecy is tainted.

Later, as Saul escalated his attempts to kill David, he enlisted others' help. God intervened, so Saul himself finally went to commit the murder. During his pursuit, Saul again prophesied, but this time when God's Spirit came upon him (see 1 Sam. 19:22-23). He stripped off his clothes and lay naked day and night. People again questioned Saul's prophesying like they had when he'd prophesied with Samuel (see 1 Sam. 19:24). However, this time they asked sarcastically. Many today call themselves prophets and give massive prophetic words. However, if their lives don't demonstrate God's high standards for His prophets, people will recognize their polluted words masked as prophecy. Constantly assessing hearts and motives must be part of a prophetic lifestyle.

Strongholds

Spiritual strongholds also have an important role in ministry. A stronghold is an area of darkness (ignorance or unbelief) in the carnal, unrenewed mind. It provides legal access for demons' thoughts and characteristics to influence a person's thought life (see 2 Pet. 2:4; Jude 6). Strongholds are pulled down when exposed to the light of God's truth. Strongholds are symbolized by the *-ites*, who held possessions in the Promised Land (see Deut. 7:1). -Ites were to be utterly destroyed—Canaanites (pride), Jebusites (depression), Amorites (accusation), Girgashites (lack of integrity), Perizzites (rebellion, no self-control), Hivites (manipulation, witchcraft), and Hittites (fear). Each enemy stronghold has spiritual implications. The Promised Land is a type of our lives in Christ; our warfare is to pull these down:

For though we walk in the flesh, we do not war according to the flesh. For the weapons of our warfare are not carnal but mighty in God for pulling down strongholds, casting down arguments and every high thing that exalts itself against the knowledge of God, bringing every thought into captivity to the obedience of Christ, and being ready to punish all disobedience when your obedience is fulfilled (2 Corinthians 10:3-6).

Having strongholds doesn't mean we aren't justified through Jesus' blood. It does mean, however, we're in the process of sanctification through renewing our minds. Strongholds can result in character flaws, including inferiority; insecurity; rejection, which turns to bitterness; pride; rebellion; lack of integrity; control and manipulation; and fear. The prophetic is derailed by these and other character flaws, such as oversensitivity to criticism, immaturity, and lack of submission. Strongholds, sometimes referred to as spiritual roots, are often the cause of emotional and physical problems, including many diseases.

When we pastored, our church was known as a spiritual first-aid station. People drove miles because they could and would get healed. The problem, though, was that weeks later, some would return with the same problems. Sometimes people seem healed or delivered only to have the problem return because of an intact spiritual root. People know only what hurts; they're rarely aware of underlying spiritual causes. Issues such as bitterness, envy, fear, rejection, and other underlying roots can cause sickness and disease. As I sought God concerning this issue, the Spirit revealed what I was doing in ministry was like plucking a dandelion's head. The flower may have been gone, but the root remained. In other words, I was seeing symptoms healed but not addressing deliverance from underlying problems. The stronghold still existed. Deliverance, or pulling down strongholds, must often precede true healing.

Immaturity

Many prophetically gifted people have a divine calling but are impetuous and immature. Spiritual teenagers don't recognize their lack of maturity and potentially create problems. They believe having a revelation from Holy Spirit gives them authority over God's delegated leadership. They're routinely rejected and wander from church to church. Their desire is to be known as God's man or woman of the hour, letting all know they're God's prophet. Their demeanor is similar to spoiled children when they don't get their way. Often, prophetically immature people enter a prophetic dueling match, each prophesying bigger and better things than the other. These dueling matches end as spiritual debacles with those in attendance leaving grieved by the obvious display of carnal pride exhibited by spiritually gifted individuals abusing God's gifts.

Second Samuel gives two excellent examples of ministry immaturity. The first is when Judah and Benjamin were at war after David was anointed Judah's king (see 2 Sam. 2:18-23). A young man named Asahel "was as fleet as a wild gazelle" (2 Sam. 2:18) and fought on David's behalf. He pursued Abner, a seasoned warrior and captain of Saul's army. Abner recognized Asahel's pursuit and warned him to turn back, saying: "Why should I strike you to the ground? How then could I face your brother Joab" (2 Sam. 2:22). Asahel refused to relent, so Abner struck him with his spear's blunt end through his stomach and out his back, causing him to die. In this example, Asahel was exceptionally gifted but lacked experience to battle a champion. Too often, spiritual teens have been baptized in Holy Spirit, memorized a few Scriptures, and seen some healings and miracles, so they think they have enough experience to begin their own ministries without seasoned mentors' wisdom. Many fall flat on their faces, never to get up again. They think God let them down when actually they acted presumptuously with no clear direction of God's timing and the equipping required for ministry.

The second example is when David's forces battled against his son Absalom's forces, which were attempting to overthrow David's kingdom (see 2 Sam. 18:19-33). Absalom was defeated and killed. Joab, David's battle commander, sought an experienced man to carry news to David. A young man, Ahimaaz, said, "Let me run now and take the news to the king, how the Lord has avenged him of his enemies" (2 Sam. 18:19). Joab said he needed a mature messenger to carry word to David. He chose a Cushite to relay the message. Ahimaaz kept begging Joab to let him run; Joab finally said, "Run" (2 Sam. 18:23). Ahimaaz was much faster and easily outran the Cushite. As he came near, a watchman called out that a messenger was approaching. Ahimaaz said, "All is well" (2 Sam. 18:28)! When David asked about Absalom's fate, Ahimaaz answered, "When Joab sent the king's servant and me your servant, I saw a great tumult, but I did not know what it was about" (2 Sam. 18:29). The complete message came when the more experienced Cushite arrived with news of Absalom's death. Here again is an example of a gifted spiritual teenager who believed he had the relevant message—a revelation of good news from battle. When given the opportunity, he couldn't deliver (prophesy) because he didn't understand the entire message, timing, or delivery method of this serious word.

Immaturity, presumption, and lack of proper spiritual protocol are the main reasons many pastors shut down prophetic gifts—they don't want to deal with drama. They often consider immature, prophetically gifted believers to be spiritual nomads, trying to take over services and causing trouble. One's ability to receive divine revelation doesn't equate to spiritual maturity nor make one a prophet. Of the respected prophets I know, many served for years as evangelists, pastors, or teachers before God called them into the prophet's ministry. In nearly every case, this maturing process took over twenty years. Most don't call themselves prophets although they operate in that calling. They know their ministry gift will make a place for them without advertising a title. Operating in the gift of prophecy shouldn't be confused with the ministry gift of the prophet (see Eph. 4:11). Prophets have great responsibilities for changing existing structures, issuing divine warnings, and preempting satan's devices. Holy Spirit's gift of prophecy is to edify, exhort, and comfort.

In using gifts in a church, know where you are and be sensitive to Holy Spirit's timing. We've been in meetings where the immature violated this principle. Too often an overly enthusiastic believer gave a message in tongues or an ill-timed prophecy, disrupted the service, and caused confusion. If you feel you're supposed to attend a certain church, explain to the leadership about your Holy Spirit walk. They can weave it together so everyone gets fed, and others can employ his/her Holy Spirit abilities. More seasoned prophetic people should help others mature and expand in their gifts. This is a rewarding and challenging aspect of ministry. I love to see people with God's fire (compassion) in their lives. As a spiritual blacksmith, I need that fire to help them shape and sharpen their spiritual weapons and tools of harvest resident through Holy Spirit. Sometimes a little wildfire accompanies the prophetic, but I'd rather see wildfire than no fire at all!

Prophetic Mandate for This Time: Elijah's Anointing

At the beginning of 2012, Holy Spirit gave me a prophetic mandate I detailed in Connie's book *The Elijah Anointing.* To summarize, Elijah received God's instructions to anoint Hazael king over Syria, Jehu king over Israel, and Elisha as his replacement prophet (see 1 Kings 19:15-17). Each has a prophetic meaning today. *Hazael* means "God has seen"[1] and represents vision or prophetic revelation. Holy Spirit desires to release a visionary anointing to the church. Jehu's anointing represents power evangelism demonstrated through Holy Spirit's power gifts. The Elisha anointing is a protégé's double anointing for the next generation of ministers.

This mandate also comes with Holy Spirit's anointing(s) to accomplish these tasks. First is the *arsonist anointing* (see 1 Kings 18:20-40). As Elijah called fire down from heaven to consume the sacrifice, God's fire will be released to consume lives with His compassion. The second anointing is the *rainmaker anointing* (see 1 Kings 18:41-46). By his word, Elijah shut up the rain and dew for over three years; then on Mt. Carmel he travailed until heavy rain commenced. The rainmaker anointing is an intercessory anointing causing spiritual reality of God's word and covenant promises to rain down on earth.

Finally, in the *whirlwind anointing* Elijah was supernaturally transported by angels from the earthly environment (see 2 Kings 2:11-12). The whirlwind anointing is to prophesy removal of manmade and demonic obstacles, problems, and messes so they're blown away by the whirlwind of Holy Spirit (see Isa. 41:15-16). This whirlwind anointing is for prophecy to change the spiritual landscape. The whirlwind displaces the antichrist system of manmade religious rules and regulations and then installs Holy Spirit's reign in men's hearts. This is God's power released through His spoken word by believers vitally connected to Him through Holy Spirit.

Conclusion

Prophecy is divine communication available to every Spirit-filled believer. Through prophecy, you partner with Holy Spirit to speak God's proceeding word as revealed through Him into earth's environment. Many prophetic words spoken to Connie and me have confirmed our ministry direction. Those spoken words helped to break through the conflicting, temporary reality of circumstances attempting to cancel God's plan.

Every battle of life revolves around what you believe and with whom you agree. Do you believe in God's covenant promises and His rhema word spoken to confirm His purpose, or do you abdicate to temporary circumstances standing in the way of the prophecy's fulfillment? Your agreement with God's word or with temporary situations determines victory or defeat. Prophecy releases faith's power to break through satan's smoke clouds of doubt and darkness. Prophecy becomes the light of God's truth piercing the darkness of ignorance and confusion. Prophecy brings elevation to live above this temporary, visible environment to gain vision to view life from an eternal perspective. Prophecy has the power to carry you through hard times and infuse staying power necessary for character development. With power comes authority and responsibility to use it with discretion and integrity.

ONE TO GROW ON: INTEGRITY

Connie

Integrity—that word has changed meaning dramatically in my years here on earth. We've long since passed days of not locking our doors or doing business with a handshake. Now lawyers sue to break unbreakable contracts and often win despite previously made agreements. Politicians aren't held accountable for their actions. Parents abdicate child-rearing responsibilities. People gauge right and wrong by fear of consequences. As the world evolves, changing our own values to fit the twenty-first century morality would be easy; but no matter how the world's standards fluctuate, God's precepts don't. Cutting corners in honesty and sin just because it's in vogue doesn't mean we should follow the crowd. God still holds Christians to a higher standard, and those who operate in the gifts are required to show even more uprightness because you represent Jesus through Holy Spirit's power.

What's Your Fruit?

Knowing that, Spirit-filled Christians must always be aware of integrity. No matter what or who else justifies shortcuts, we don't answer to those who measure right and wrong by human standards. We're the chozeh, and "to whom much is given, from him much will be required; and to whom much has been committed, of him they will ask the more" (Luke 12:48). Our lives are watched, so we don't have excess wiggle room. Many who have forgotten they're separated have fallen. Though we all make character mistakes, we should live daily judging our lives by God's commandments. Paul told us "to walk worthy of the calling with which you were called" (Eph. 4:1). What do people think of when they say your name? Honesty, integrity, godliness? Some people can hear from God amazingly, but their lives are ambivalent toward Him. They choose to walk after fleshly lusts and then be godly when that suits them. That double-mindedness makes those already leery of the prophetic even warier. If we think so little of this gift that we're not willing to leave carnal lusts behind, do we truly want God's deeper things? Are we walking worthy of that calling?

I believe that's why God said, "Jacob I have loved, but Esau I have hated" (Rom. 9:13). Jacob lied, cheated, and wrestled with an angel to get the Father's blessings. Esau thought so little of his inheritance he sold it for soup. How much do you cherish the Father's gifts? Do you want them more than that relationship or job that causes compromise? You should constantly assess your life. If something isn't right, don't stay out of church because maintaining Christian fellowship helps you get solid. However, take yourself temporarily from leadership and the prophetic stance. Even being lukewarm reflects badly on God and you and makes others lose confidence in the prophetic.

Beware

Prophetic people fall into traps that can affect their hearing from God or influence others receiving the word. One is neglect of our gift. Ezekiel says God has, "made you a watchman for the house of Israel; therefore you shall hear a word from [His] mouth and warn them for [Him]" (Ezek. 33:7). Our mouths speak God's warnings because you and I are watchers, but we sometimes neglect that responsibility. Acting on a word from God is crucial because others might suffer when we don't treat God's revelations as our important assignment.

Once, during a Sunday night service when I was a teen, I had a vision of my sister Lynda riding in a convertible. I described her as she was in the vision—fringe bangs, curly ponytail, and specific clothes. When I told the vision, the church had an obligatory prayer. Had I been older both chronologically and in my gifts, I would have insisted they take this seriously, but I learned the hard way. The next weekend, someone returned from vacation with a terrible story. She'd been in heavy interstate traffic when a carload of teenagers whisked by. She noticed a girl in front who looked exactly like Lynda—hair fixed how I'd seen and wearing what I'd described. Suddenly, traffic stopped; our friend inched through the jam until she saw the problem. That convertible full of teens had wrecked; the girl who looked like Lynda was lying there, decapitated. Even if others don't take us seriously, we should be diligent. We're watchers, so being slothful is disobedience.

Another thing we need to watch is pride. God hates arrogance and pride (see Prov. 18:13), which make us neglect to give Him credit. Because He deserves glory, we can't fall into the trap of thinking we can do anything on our own. Peter says:

> If anyone speaks, let him speak as the oracles of God. If anyone ministers, let him do it as with the ability which God supplies, that in all things God may be glorified through Jesus Christ, to whom belong the glory and the dominion forever and ever (1 Peter 4:11).

We don't receive revelations, healings, or miracles through our ability. Try as I might, I can't make Holy Spirit's gifts happen. When I realize I can do all things through God, it's a sure thing His ability will bring results for His glory, not mine.

Another trap prophetic people fall into is desiring personal acknowledgement—to be seen, gain wealth, or make a name. In Acts 16, a possessed slave girl following Paul and Silas wanted to be seen. She kept yelling that they were men of God. At times, groupies follow prophetic people for vicarious acknowledgement. We might be flattered when someone elevates us, but it's a distraction from our godly purpose. The disciples grew tired of her and cast out demons.

Another time, Elisha's servant, Gehazi, demonstrated an example of how greed crept into a ministry (see 2 Kings 5:20-24). Elisha had performed the miracle of Naaman's healing from leprosy but refused his offer of riches. However, Gehazi longed for that money. He returned to Naaman in Elisha's name, asked for the money, received it, then lied to Elisha. Through a word of knowledge, Elisha said:

> *Did not my heart go with you when the man turned back from his chariot to meet you? Is it time to receive money and to receive clothing, olive groves and vineyards, sheep and oxen, male and female servants?* (2 Kings 5:26)

What a sad story on many levels. Gehazi had seen what God could do, but he still harbored greed then allowed God's works to be part of a bartering process. As Elisha told him, Naaman's healing wasn't done so they could receive riches or accumulate things. Unlike the human mindset, God's prophets don't give with the end goal of receiving. Because of his wrong motives and actions, Gehazi paid a high price—not only did he lose his mentor's trust and his own opportunity to be Elisha's protégé, but Naaman's leprosy afflicted him. Ministries are derailed because they become businesses needing to operate their own way rather than following God's direction, which might affect their bottom line. God will provide what we need, and we shouldn't sell our services to make it happen.

False Prophecy

In whatever we do, we should be cautious about whom we trust—the used car salesman with that perfect lemon, the seller of our amazing dream house, the surgeon who gives a bad report, the man/woman of our dreams. Life is filled with charlatans who take advantage by misrepresenting themselves. Unfortunately, the prophetic also has people who want to be revered but are false. Moses (see Deut. 13:1-3), Jeremiah, (see Jer. 14:14), Micah (see Mic. 3:5-7), and others warned of them. As Jesus said, "Let your 'Yes' be 'Yes,' and your 'No,' 'No'"

(Matt. 5:37); our words should always be true whether we deal daily life or prophetic pronouncements. Ahab's prophets' lies ca. his death as they predicted success in a battle that actually spel ... defeat for Israel (see 1 Kings 22:23). False prophets often are like most of Ahab's—not evil but immature in operating in their gifts, presumptive in believing wrongly they've heard from God, or self-serving because they have personal motives. A prophet's job is to give only what God says and judge what's false or real by looking at ours and others' integrity, motivations, and fruit.

Jeremiah gave scenarios of false prophets. In chapter 28, Hananiah gave a prophecy refuting Jeremiah's because he had a motive to gratify his countrymen, desperate for deliverance from their invaders' bondage. He gave three false promises: (1) God would break Babylon's yoke from Judah, (2) vessels Nebuchadnezzar stole from God's house would be returned within two years, and (3) the Prince of Judah would come back to Judah. He punctuated this word by physically breaking a yoke off Jeremiah's neck. I understand how he wanted to speak encouraging words to desperate people and why they welcomed his promises with great rejoicing. However, prophets can't be people-pleasers. Jeremiah wasn't driven by any motivation other than saying what God spoke. He prophesied that because of Hananiah's false word, instead of wood, the yoke would now be iron, and beasts of the field would serve King Nebuchadnezzar. His prophecy was right; Hananiah died seven months later. Giving a word pleasing to others looking for hope is popular; but unless God says it, it's false prophecy.

In chapter 29, Jeremiah and other prophets were again challenged but this time to eliminate true prophets and priests and replace them with counterfeit ones. In this chapter, Shemaiah probably resented Jeremiah's and others' prophetic abilities. He undermined, persecuted, then promoted rebellion against them and God. Shemaiah sent letters to Jerusalem and to Zephaniah the priest to rebuke those prophets, put them and true priests into stocks, and label them as "demented" for declaring a long Babylonian captivity (Jer. 29:26). True words may be challenged by false prophets who play on others' needs to hear good reports and forget God's harsh judgment. Because of Shemaiah's pleasant words, people trusted a lie and rebelled against Jeremiah. As punishment, God banished Shemaiah and his family and didn't allow them to see the future good God did.

One word of caution, though. Before you judge others' prophetic words as false, know that sometimes you just don't understand the whole picture. Matthew 2 exemplifies how you may judge wrongly when actually a word is truly from God. Matthew tells that prophets said Jesus would come from "Bethlehem of Judea" (Matt 2:5), "out of Egypt" (Matt. 2:15), and "in a city called Nazareth…[and would be] called a Nazarene" (Matt. 2:23). Imagine that! Within a few verses, Matthew gives a wide variety of prophecies spoken about the Messiah. They all came to pass; and even though each message varied greatly in prophetic content, none were false. The hearer was probably skeptical because of seeming contradictions; but that was from lack of understanding on his part, not the prophet's. I've heard too many people throw around the term "false prophet" when actually that word was right on. Let the Spirit and Scripture lead you to truth, and don't summarily dismiss something you don't understand.

Envy

Often, those who challenge prophetic words from God are driven by envy. If you haven't encountered that because of your gifts, you will. Many envy others' gifts and closeness to God but don't invest in what's necessary to find that intimacy. Actually, "where envy and self-seeking exist, confusion and every evil thing are there" (James 3:16). Envy is an aspect of someone's being self-centered instead of Christ-centered. Focusing on oneself opens the door for "every evil thing" to come into lives. Envy because of a brother's gifts, talents, or relationship with the Father goes back to Cain and Abel or to Joseph, whose coat demonstrated his father's favor. In both these examples, it was a brother, not a heathen, who exhibited envy. Does that speak to you? I once heard a preacher say Joseph knew his brothers were envious of his many-colored coat, but he wore it anyway because it was a gift from the father. What an amazing way to view your gifts. No matter how others react, those gifts are Holy Spirit conceived, birthed, nurtured, and refined. They're bestowed specially from the Father to you.

I love David's response to Saul's envy. Though he was anointed by Samuel to be king and God's Spirit had departed from Saul, David respected that office during the season in which God was preparing him to rule. No matter how Saul persecuted him, "David behaved wisely in all his ways, and the Lord was with him" (1 Sam. 18:14). Ironically, even though David "behaved wisely," Saul's reaction was fear, not respect for David's wisdom and anointing (see 1 Sam. 18:15). As often happens, David was then confused about Saul's attempts to murder him when he had done only good things for Saul and Israel. He wondered, "What have I done? What is my iniquity…, what is my sin?" (1 Sam. 20:1).

That reaction mirrors our response when we've been good to people who inexplicably turn on us. It's simply about envy for our anointing. Although we'd like to seek retribution, instead we should imitate David. He wasn't responsible for Saul's actions; but he had every obligation to use wisdom in *his* ways—his respect for Saul's office, his building relationships with future subjects, his growing in intimacy with God, his living circumspectly before men and the Father. As God takes you deeper into your gifts, your preparation season and reactions to others will determine how far God can promote you.

Receiving Our Words

Another integrity issue is how prophetic people take rejection. Some think others should jump on their every word and get offended when they give a word that someone doesn't act on. Our job isn't to change or manipulate others. We're to be obedient then let God take over and do His changing and directing. When Paul visited Philip's house in Caesarea (see Acts 21:9-14), Agabus had a prophetic word for him. He bound Paul's hands and feet with his girdle, which represented how he would be arrested at Jerusalem. Paul heard the prophecy and saw sad reactions from the group but declared he was going anyway. This story speaks to those who operate in the prophetic. Obviously, Agabus could hear from God because everyone reacted to this word with weeping; his prophecy did come to pass in Jerusalem. However, just because he said it, Paul wasn't obligated to act on it. Like Agabus, we're to say what God gives then let receivers of the word do what they feel led to do. Their opinions or actions aren't a negative reflection on us.

Besides, no one should base decisions solely on another's words. Each revelation is one piece of a God-crafted puzzle and must be judged because even our own words may be flawed on some level— misinterpretation, wrong timing, the hearer's misunderstanding. Our responsibility is sharing the word. The receiver's obedience is between him and God, not him and us. We can't be offended if someone dismisses, verbally challenges, or even ridicules us because those things happen to everyone. Offense changes Holy Spirit's purpose. By the same token, we should watch how we receive words from others, too. We should not only test others' spirits (see 1 John 4:1), but we should also test the revelation's validity with our own spirits and the Word. We should weigh theirs, like they should weigh ours. Especially when a young Christian gives a word, we should receive with an open mind then be led by God. People have missed out on great blessings when they rejected the message because of the messenger.

Obedience

Another trap prophetic people can fall into is not doing things how God said. He doesn't need to justify or explain His whys or wherefores. His ways are perfect, so we must do it just how He says—with His words and timing, to the right people, at the right place, in the right tone, with the right love. Just like with our own children, He gives us time to grow up; but the more we mature, our wiggle room diminishes. We know His voice intimately, so we should speak on His behalf and do things His way to represent His heart. Moses learned that the hard way. In Horeb, they had no water; so God gave His plan—if he would strike a rock, water would come forth (see Exod. 17:6). He did, and it flowed abundantly. It was logical then, with no water in the Desert of Zin in Kadesh, that Moses should again strike the rock. After all, it had worked the last time. Water erupted but at a great price. Though he'd done many good things in the past, this action prohibited him from entering the Promised Land because he'd disobeyed God by striking it instead of speaking to it (see Num. 20:1-13). God doesn't add up our good and bad columns and give us a pass when we disobey. Can we learn from Moses that doing things God's way is crucial? He expects His frontline generals to have learned the unquestioning-obedience lesson.

Another story shows drastic consequences for disobedience. In First Kings 13, a man of God travelled from Judah to give a word to King Jeroboam, who became angry about this negative word. He stretched his hand against the man of God; it withered, and the altar split. Jeroboam repented, so God restored both. When Jeroboam tried to bless him with food, the man refused because God had said not to eat or drink in Bethel. However, on his way home, an old prophet stopped him and said an angel had sent him to bring the man of God back for food. After he'd eaten, the old prophet gave another word that his guest would be killed because he'd disobeyed God. Although that old prophet was revered enough for the man of God to follow his directions even after refusing the king, a prophet's words can be flawed for whatever motive. We must do what God said even though a trusted person says an angel told him and our bellies are growling from hunger. This man of God was killed by a lion on the way home.

Our Opinions

This story tells another lesson we must watch—presenting opinions as if they're from God. This is easy to do because we all have them, and sometimes separating those from our gift is hard. The old prophet had an opinion that he confused with God's message and then pronounced it authoritatively. If we think our revelation is right but aren't 100 percent sure, we should keep quiet or say, "This could just be me, but…" and distinguish between what we know and what we think, giving only His unembellished words. Sometimes, people look to us to interpret or give direction. If we don't have the revelation or interpretation, we can't create one. Our opinions matter, especially since we have Christ's mind, and people seek us for that wisdom. However, we should differentiate between opinion and Holy Spirit's revelation.

One specific way people fall into the opinion trap is when they confuse what they've deduced through logic with what Holy Spirit revealed. Some give words just because something they witnessed made them draw a conclusion; then they present that as a word from God. Those people prophesy from their carnal mind, rather than from the Spirit. Also, giving your own opinion as if it's from the Lord in order to manipulate is a big pitfall. We used to know a wonderful minister who could hear from God, but she also tried to control people. Her opinion became mixed with her prophetic gift, so she had difficulty separating it because she became accustomed to telling people what to do and having them do it. Controlling others is wrong, and our gifts aren't for that purpose. No one is perfect in his/her gifts all the time, but you must be willing to change when your error is revealed, or "Woe to the foolish prophets, who follow their own spirit and have seen nothing" (Ezek. 13:3)! Consequences may not be as drastic as a lion on the road, but our words will create a penalty for both us and the person receiving the prophecy.

Love

Every gift operates through love, humility, and integrity. Jesus personifies love, so each time you move in the Spirit should be motivated from that stance. Paul is specific about how the gifts are to be used. In 1 Corinthians 12, he lists them. Then in 1 Corinthians 14 he explains how tongues and prophecy work. The chapter in between, First Corinthians 13, is about the greatest gift—love. Love makes gifts operate properly. Holy Spirit gives these tools for building, not tearing down. Just as preachers shouldn't use the logos to beat someone up, neither should those who receive rhemas. However, as I said earlier, you shouldn't avoid giving "hard" words. Sometimes, you may be the tool God uses to set someone on the right path because a word given in love will accomplish what another cannot.

Wade and I were preaching in the South when a man came to the service. In the Spirit, I saw him cruising in a convertible, his arm resting on the door like he was sixteen and without a care. The Lord said to me, "It's time you grow up in Me." I didn't know him and didn't want to say something potentially hurtful, but I knew God was speaking to me. In the love of a sister who wanted her brother to grow, I told him what I'd seen. That man readily received because God had been speaking to him about plunging into Holy Spirit. That night, he was filled with the Spirit and truly began his deeper, more "grown up" walk.

Operating in love also makes us observe another integrity issue— keeping prophetic revelations in confidence. Solomon spoke about watching our mouths and that "a talebearer reveals secrets, but he who is of a faithful spirit conceals a matter" (Prov. 11:13). That goes double for revealing God's secrets. He also says we should keep even personal disputes private because it's shameful and will affect our reputations (see Prov. 25:9-10). That tells me I need to keep my mouth closed when I tell others about a situation so I can vent or justify myself. Giving too much information about our lives or telling another's secrets reflects badly on God, us, and our ministries. Reputation is important, especially when we're about the Father's business.

Recognizing Levels of Authority

Another prophetic issue that shows integrity is how each person, even prophets, submits to the church's authority. Some people can never move into their destiny because they haven't learned that lesson. Even if you hear from God 100 percent better than your pastor, it's not your job to thwart his authority. Remember David and Saul? David's submission to the king from whom the anointing had departed shows that though you're anointed for a particular office, you can't move there at leadership's expense. I've heard people say, "If my God gives me a word, I'm gonna give it no matter what anybody says!" That's rebellion. Yes, you should somehow find a way to share God's revelation, but that doesn't mean you interrupt the service's flow, are obligated even to give it during the service, or go against the pastor's wishes. By God's design, the pastor, not the prophet, is in charge and determines who shares what. When God gives a revelation either at our home church or at another assembly where we don't how they feel about the gifts, Wade writes it down and hands the paper to an usher. Then we're obedient while observing godly order. If the pastor acts on it, great; if he doesn't, we've obeyed.

When you do find liberty to move, you should learn how and when to flow. Even in a congregation that operates in the gifts, do so in an orderly way and observe God's timing. Sometimes I've shared revelations too soon and broken the service's flow. To keep that from happening, you should remember that you're not the only member of the body who can hear from God, so sometimes you need to wait to see if someone else has the appropriate move. If God wants you to share during the service, He'll provide an opportunity. When it seems there's no place to share, ask God for an opening.

Usually, if I diligently watch, I can find a small window to jump in. If I don't get the chance, after church, I still try to be faithful to act on that revelation. I tell the pastor what I saw or go to the person for whom I had a message. Then I've done my best to obey the Lord while still observing protocol. Your gift isn't an uncontrollable steamroller that can't be harnessed but rather "the spirits of the prophets are subject to the prophets" (1 Cor. 14:32). Holy Spirit doesn't force you to give; you're able to control when, where, and if you act on that message. The Spirit never compels someone to be out of order. He knows how to get His message across and still work within Kingdom procedures.

Handling Mistakes

Part of growing in the gifts is making mistakes. A prophetic person won't succeed unless he/she is willing to make mistakes. And you will! Remember the man who gave me a word about my finger rather than my toe? Imperfect people, including you and me, give imperfect words; so instead of being crippled by mistakes, get up and try again. To mature in Holy Spirit, people must practice their gifts and make errors without condemnation. Nobody should batter someone because he/she was wrong but rather should encourage that person because he/she had the fortitude to try.

More seasoned operators should mentor and direct fledgling prophets to do better next time. Whether the mistake is speaking out of turn, giving a wrong word, or not speaking at all, you learn over time. If it's a mistake not motivated by integrity issues, God can work with a teachable, contrite spirit. As with all things, errors can be stumbling blocks or stepping stones, depending on your attitude. If they're your foe, they can end your Holy Spirit operation. As your friend, they can launch you toward God's blessings and greater revelations. The attitudes of those who've made the mistake and others' reactions determine where new users of the gifts go from there.

I began operating in the gifts before I was a teenager. Some said unkind things to me when I made my many mistakes. Those who criticized instead of instructed could have discouraged me so much I might have stopped trying. However, more people helped than hurt me, and they showed me how to use those mistakes in my newly acquired gifts to do better the next time. Where I am today is in large part due to those encouragers. Some have devastated prophets-in-training, while others have encouraged and brought them into an amazing prophetic voice. Which do you want to be, encourager or destroyer? Anyone who says you can't make errors in this prophetic walk doesn't understand that like everything else in your Christian journey, learning to use the gifts is a progression. Blunders are usually not integrity-based. They're made by believers who are learning about their gifts and making plain ole' mistakes!

Conclusion

When I was teenager, my siblings and I played practical jokes on one another. One day, one sister and I decided to play a trick on an irritating younger sister. We made up a scenario and told that sister that I had a dream about her. We planned to set the record straight eventually; but before we could, the victim of the prank told people at church about the dream and asked for their help interpreting it. I was forced to confess I'd made it up—right there in front of people I loved, esteemed, and wanted their respect. As humiliating as that was, my duplicity was discovered in just the right way for me to know that what I did was terrible! I could take lightly any manner of things, but a gift from Holy Spirit was to be revered higher than anything else. Even nearly fifty years later, though I know God doesn't condemn, I'm still regretful and embarrassed I did such a bad thing with such a precious gift.

Holy Spirit entrusted our giftings to us and expects us to use them properly—not for gain, to receive a name for ourselves, to speak our minds, to exert manipulation, or to play a joke on a younger sister. As we mature, we realize that along with being the chozeh comes intense responsibility. Integrity determines how deeply we grow in God and how *not* to be a blemish to Him. People look up to those who operate in the gifts and expect us to hear from God, so we must keep our lives in line and our gifts in perspective. We're part of the body, and our gifts work in tandem with the rest of our body. Whether it's our conduct or our gifts, we affect each other. And that, my friend, is just how it is.

Part III

POWER GIFTS

POWER GIFTS

Wade

Natural warfare requires application of superior, concentrated air and ground power to destroy the enemy. Any nation neglecting its military might opens a door for enemy attack. Military power is essential to living in freedom from oppression and tyranny. History is filled with examples of nations that ceased to exist because they neglected defenses and were overpowered by enemies. This principle applies to spiritual power. Unfortunately, much of the church has equivocated Holy Spirit's role with no revelations of His power for believers to live free of satan's devices. Therefore, they live in bondage to the evil one when they have God's power available to destroy his works through Holy Spirit's weapons.

Power—this word can be intimidating. Power (dunamis) differentiates what's of God's Kingdom or man's. Paul wrote, "For the kingdom of God is not in word but in power" (1 Cor. 4:20). Men's works fall short when compared to God's power manifested through the Spirit. I've heard believers describe power gifts as spooky, weird, and unbelievable; yet, these gifts are sought by those needing healing, financial help, or creative miracles. God's purposes on earth won't be fully manifested until believers understand their roles in cooperation with Holy Spirit in power gifts. Nothing demonstrates God's agape like the operation of power gifts—faith, gifts of healings, and working of miracles.

Compassion

Perhaps the most important ingredient in power gifts is compassion. Throughout the Gospels, whenever Jesus was moved with compassion, acts of power were demonstrated. Masses healed (see Matt. 9:35-36), miracles provided (see Matt. 15:32), blinded eyes opened (see Matt. 20:34), lepers cleansed (see Mark 1:41), demons cast out (see Mark 5:19), dead raised (see Luke 7:13)—all were results of Jesus being moved with compassion. It's an irresistible force against the devil's wiles and earth's cursed condition. Paul spoke of compassion when he used the phrases, "the bowels of Jesus Christ" and "bowels and mercies" (Phil. 1:8; 2:1 KJV). I like these descriptions, which bring to mind a deep gnawing in our innermost being demanding movement. Compassion moved Jesus to acts of power directed against the enemy to destroy his works (see 1 John 3:8).

I define compassion as the firstborn of the union of God's agape love married to His wrath against satan and what sin has done to His creation—man. Compassion is a perfect mixture of God's love for us and fury against His enemies. It's an accelerant activating power gifts of healings and working of miracles. Today, some mistake pity for compassion. Pity's a poor substitute, even a counterfeit, for compassion because it's a powerless, futile gesture offering nothing to change a cursed condition. Pity is similar to complaint—both indicate language and actions of powerless people.

Compassion, on the other hand, is God's fire that destroys the devil's works through a release of heaven's lightning power on His enemies. Imagine Jesus braiding a whip and driving money changers from His Father's temple. That was compassion at work. Jesus healing all who came to Him, raising the widow's dead son, and praying over bread and fishes that multiplied were acts of compassion working through miracles. True compassion is too expensive for most Laodicean, lukewarm believers (see Rev. 3:14-16).

Compassion comes with a tremendous price—Jesus' blood applied to sin. Without this ultimate display of compassion, humanity would remain in a lost condition. When we declared Jesus is Lord, we didn't just change our lives; we exchanged our old life for His new life. We're not our own; we've been purchased with a price—God's very *compassion*. If we're truly His, we'll become like Him—full of compassion for others. Compassion goes beyond selfish needs and desires and secures God's blessings for others. Maybe we've become too jaded to be moved by others' infirmities. Jesus ministered with compassion, and we're to access God's power as well as His covenant promises. Our mission is to transfer those promises into this natural realm and direct them into life's messes. Compassion is the force that accelerates this process.

Power

Because of weakness, lack of knowledge, and unbelief, the church has allowed the enemy to foist his banner of destruction over many parts of our nation. This has made the church irrelevant in the world's eyes. We've relinquished spiritual authority and power in the name of political correctness by trying hard not to offend. Now most Christians "have a form of godliness but [deny] its power" (2 Tim. 3:5). It's time for the church (us) to rise up in Holy Spirit's power to reverse sin's curse for which we've been given God's spiritual authority (see Gen. 1:26, Matt. 28:18-20). That's Holy Spirit's purpose—to manifest Kingdom reality (see Matt. 6:10) and demonstrate God's love through His might! Power gifts work as a demonstration of God's heart of love.

The gifts are a powerful kingdom force similar to electricity—a life-changing power source in society. We're familiar with the standard 110-volt power from most home outlets. Today, we take it for granted; we flip a switch and light instantly comes on—that is, until a power outage occurs. Imagine living in the days of coal-oil lanterns or candles, without TVs, computers, electric stoves, microwaves, and other modern conveniences. That's exactly what living without Holy Spirit's power is like for many churches today—they exist by the candlelight of a reflection of a past move of Holy Spirit, not in the present illumination of His person. Power gifts turn on lights. Like electricity, God's power is extremely beneficial when properly used; but if we don't understand the rules of electricity, we can suffer shock, serious injury, or worse! Similar spiritual damage can occur from abuse of power gifts as well. Because of this extreme divine force, believers must be careful about abuses of these gifts.

FAITH

Wade

Repetitious military training is required so actions under stress and extreme conditions (i.e., enemy fire) become second nature. This rigorous training regimen develops a mission-oriented mindset to press forward with little regard for self. Despite barriers and enemy resistance, heroic feats of valor often result from this training. The gift of faith also relies on rigorous attention to the Word of God and Holy Spirit's weapons. Through use, faith ultimately becomes second nature. Faith has power to accomplish the impossible in the face of overwhelming obstacles. The gift of faith is imparted under extreme conditions when confronted with seemingly unconquerable situations and goes beyond simple faith's potential to bring about miraculous results.

The progression of the gift of faith often operates like this:

- We spend time praying in the Spirit (tongues).
- Holy Spirit reveals words of knowledge, words of wisdom, and discernment of spirits.
- We announce what Holy Spirit revealed (speaking gifts).
- People respond to revelations by coming forward to receive prayer or by performing prophetic actions. The gift of faith, in cooperation with gifts of healings and working of miracles, brings about deliverance, healings, and creative miracles.

The gift of faith works in conjunction with other power gifts—gifts of healings and working of miracles. Most often, this gift begins with divine revelation—a word of knowledge or word of wisdom. When one knows Holy Spirit's mind, the gift of faith flows into the situation with healings, miracles, signs and wonders following.

Gift of Faith Results

My first experience with the gift of faith was as a beneficiary of its results. In 1974, I resigned my commission as an army officer and began a new career. In the interim, I spent time with my family in Indiana. During that period, I attended our country church. As was my usual custom, that hot summer Sunday morning I slid into a back-row pew. A strange Filipino lady spoke that morning. Her English wasn't very good, so understanding her was difficult. That was the least of her strangeness, though.

During that morning service, she stopped and spoke to the whole congregation in her clipped accent, "Someone here has a terrible headache. If you'll come forward, God will heal you." Well, we'd never heard anything like that and had no idea God could heal; so of course, no one went forward. That wasn't done in our church. Everyone looked around, but no one responded. Not even me. Despite my head nearly bursting from pain, I wouldn't budge from my seat.

My mother, recently baptized in Holy Spirit, was responsible for bringing that lady to our church. The previous night, she'd been in a Full Gospel service where the woman was ministering. During service, she stated (word of wisdom) that she'd be ministering in a Presbyterian church the next morning. My mother knew ours was the only one in the county, and this lady wouldn't be appreciated by the pastor or congregation. She'd tried to slip out of the meeting, but circumstances forced her to invite the lady to stay at my parents' house and go to our church the next morning.

After preaching that morning, she came to our farmhouse for lunch, the typical custom with any visiting minister. She kept staring at me during the meal, somehow knowing my condition. I was in such pain I couldn't finish eating, so I lay down. Even then, I didn't improve but felt like my head was in a vise. I later found out that was due to my brain swelling. I couldn't think, see well, tolerate light, or do anything without excruciating pain. My RN sister recognized my condition and insisted I go to the hospital. Diagnosed with viral meningitis, I needed an immediate spinal tap to relieve brain pressure or sustain permanent damage. My family panicked. Others they'd known who'd been afflicted by this malady had been permanently disabled or had died.

As fear gripped my mother, that Filipino lady grabbed her hand and began praying for healing and restoration. She asked Mom, "Can you believe God for your son's healing?"

Mom just looked at her. Finally, she answered, "I don't know." Still holding her hand, the missionary prayed for faith to be deposited into my mother. As those words left her mouth, something changed. Mom received the gift of faith as Holy Spirit dropped it into her spirit. By human logic, I was in terrible shape and maybe dying, but Mom knew I'd be okay. She declared I was healed and refused to visit me in the hospital because *she knew I was healed.*

My sister, though, was livid. "Your son's on his deathbed," she told her, "and you won't even go see him! If you don't wake up, there'll be men in white suits carrying you off to the insane asylum." My mother just shook her head, stood her ground, and refused to doubt God's promise because of the gift of faith deposited within her. When the gift of faith comes, nothing can tell you otherwise. That was the case this time too. I was out of the hospital later that evening! As God deposited healing into my body, that day He also placed a hunger into me to better know this miracle-working God.

The gift of faith for operation of power gifts is much like faith required for salvation or any other promise of God, only more pro-nounced. It goes beyond common faith expectations. Holy Spirit authors this gift of faith and drops it into a believing heart, creat-ing power within to release Kingdom manifestation for healing and creative miracles. Our part is to stand and believe the work's been accomplished. Those most often experiencing the gift of faith know Scriptures, live them, and have developed a sensitive spiritual ear to hear the Spirit speaking. Romans 10:17 says, "So then faith comes by hearing, and hearing by the word of God." This refers to God's spoken word (rhema), which comes as Holy Spirit's revelation. When He releases rhema into a believer's heart, that word carries the gift of faith with it to cause manifestations. Revelation often initiates it, and rhema transports the gift of faith that causes the word to manifest.

Faith

Many wonderful books have been written about faith. Great faith teachers and preachers have advanced and caused the spiritual water level of faith to rise. The charismatic renewal in the seventies caused tremendous Holy Spirit growth to flow beyond Pentecostal and Full Gospel circles, who already knew Holy Spirit's power and presence, into mainstream denominations. Baptists, Lutherans, Methodists, Catholics, and Presbyterians were swept into this mighty Holy Spirit move.

Spiritually growing up during this time, I witnessed tremendous healings and miracles. I also encountered poor faith teaching by people with no real Holy Spirit experience, just a zeal for the Lord. Because of this teaching, many young believers developed a formula relationship with God—"If I do this in the proper sequence, God is obligated to provide my desires." Obviously, this left many immature believers soured on faith teaching because God didn't comply by giving them a new Cadillac or big estate they'd claimed. They assumed that simply declaring then believing for desires would somehow make them appear. That's the story of the genie from a bottle, not Jesus of the Bible. This teaching became known as "name it and claim it" or "gab it and grab it." No real faith was exercised, only some metaphysical mantra, which is witchcraft. True faith is based on God's Word and operates by His Kingdom principles. God will never violate His own principles.

Faith is one such principle, based on expectation of His covenant promises manifesting:

> *Now faith is the substance of things hoped for, the evidence of things not seen...But without faith it is impossible to please Him, for he who comes to God must believe that He is, and that He is a rewarder of those who diligently seek Him* (Hebrews 11:1, 6).

Faith results require one to hope and believe without yet seeing evidence because he/she operates in the Spirit realm where "all the promises of God in Him are Yes, and in Him Amen, to the glory of God through us" (2 Cor. 1:20). In other words, when God speaks a word, that rhema result is created and established in the invisible Spirit realm. Faith then becomes the bridge that spans the chasm between the Spirit and natural realms. As believers of God's word, we're transfer agents, carrying the manifestation over faith's bridge by first believing, then speaking, and finally acting on the word.

Door of Faith

Jesus tells how that's done in what I consider the hallmark faith Scripture, which defines two elements necessary for faith's operation:

> *Have faith in God. For assuredly, I say to you, whoever says to this mountain, "Be removed and be cast into the sea," and does not doubt in his heart, but believes that those things he says will be done, he will have whatever he says. Therefore I say to you, whatever things you ask when you pray, believe that you receive them, and you will have them* (Mark 11:22-24).

Two hinges exist on the door of faith—believing and speaking. To operate, both hinges must be in place. Believing alone won't manifest a faith result because it must be followed by action—and speaking is action. God spoke and created, as do we who are created in His image and according to His likeness (see Gen. 1:26). Believing the word causes spiritual conception, which Jesus described in the sower parable as seed, *sperma*, ("something sown, i.e. *seed* [including the male '*sperm*']; by impl. *offspring*; spec. *a remnant* [fig. as if kept over for planting]; issue")[1] (see Mark 4:14-20). As we believe, we conceive God's Word. Having conceived, we now speak from the reality of the Word's spiritual substance within us. We don't speak to get something from God but from already having received in the Spirit. By speaking, we cause the spiritual reality to manifest in the natural.

Another important aspect of faith is visualization, for we should "see" the manifestation before it becomes reality. God showed Abram stars in the sky and told him his descendants would outnumber them; he could visualize God's promise as he looked up. Abram "believed in the Lord, and He accounted it to him for righteousness" (Gen. 15:5-6). God told Joshua, "See! I have given Jericho into your hand, its king, and all the mighty men of valor" (Josh. 6:2). We should visualize the word working.

This spiritual concept occurred when Jacob made a deal with his uncle and father-in-law Laban to receive his own herds of various markings. Jacob stripped bark from branches and put them into the solid-colored goats' troughs. When they peered into that trough to drink, they visualized stripes, spots, and streaks then produced striped, spotted, and streaked offspring. Jacob left his in-laws as a wealthy man (see Gen. 30:25-43). If this principle of visualization worked for goats, it will certainly work for us! Where no revelation (vision) exists, faith results probably won't occur (see Prov. 29:18). Revelation and visions are portraits of our future—what we hope for and expect to receive. Faith is the spiritual force that reaches into our future and pulls our vision into our present situation. Faith and vision are divinely connected to one another.

Conclusion

Connie's mother and father, Audrey and Ernest Hunter, were people of faith who trusted God for their family. During the years of bringing up their eight children, many times God deposited the gift of faith into Audrey for her young children, but they didn't discover the results until years later. For example, when Connie was in kindergarten and college, her smallpox vaccinations didn't take. When doctors told her she had a natural immunity, her mom remembered when God had healed her from smallpox as an infant. Another time, Connie's brother, Phillip, cut off his fingertip in the door. Audrey took the finger, anointed it with oil, and wrapped a Band-Aid around it. It healed perfectly!

Another incident came to light a few years ago. Connie went for X-rays after an injury to her arm. When the doctor came to read the films, he looked surprised. "This arm's been busy."

Connie just laughed. "Yep, I broke it three times when I was a kid."

The doctor shook his head. "No. There are four old breaks." He pointed them out.

When Connie asked her mom about that extra break, she said, "Hmm. I thought it was broken." Then she told of how when Connie was young, she'd hurt her arm one morning. Though the arm was obviously fractured, Audrey received that gift of faith which said Connie would be all right. She rubbed anointing oil on it and put it in a sling. By the afternoon, Connie had discarded the sling and was using that arm to play with the other kids.

Galatians 6:9 provides the principle of eventuality: "And let us not grow weary while doing good, for in due season we shall reap if we do not lose heart." Having believed and conceived, then spoken and visualized the word operating, we're assured of eventual manifestation. Our part is to stand firm, not grow weary, and not lose faith while waiting on the manifestation. Praising God for His promise and worshiping Him hastens His answers. Once, as I was questioning God about His timing in providing His promised harvest, I heard Holy Spirit say, "When the reaping is later, the harvest is greater." Don't lose heart. The bigger the promise, the more diligent and fervent must be our stand on His word by faith (see Eph. 6:10-17).

GIFTS OF HEALINGS

Connie

We receive numerous requests for prayer—legal problems, custody issues, marital difficulties, loved ones' salvations, deliverance. The list's lengthiness pales, though, in comparison to our most requested prayer need—healing. We believe in healing, not just as a maybe-it'll-happen concept but as a real occurrence God does regularly. Faith for those healings and miracles was planted in me as a child. I never forgot the reality that formed in me beneath those big-top tents when our parents took us Hunter kids to see healing evangelists. Since Wade and I started in the ministry, we've seen God heal everything from belly buttons to cancer because that's who He is—a Healer. The problem with writing about healing in one chapter of a Holy Spirit book is the difficulty of explaining the basics so you'll understand your gift. Healing covers volumes.

God cares about not only our spiritual man but also our bodies. Because healing is so personal, much of Jesus' ministry was devoted to it. As those in need pursued and pushed in around the Great Physician, He showed that healing isn't just available but part of our covenant promises. In this book, you've read many examples from our own ministry of Holy Spirit's work. Healing is something every human has needed or will need in his/her life, so knowing how to appropriate it is crucial. As I've written this book, I've realized that power gifts are different from other Holy Spirit gifts. Understanding that distinction allows us warriors to live victoriously.

151

They're Different

The revelation and speaking gifts operate through a more basic level of faith—you receive, recognize the revelation is from God, and then share it. When you have a word of knowledge, you just get it. When you see a vision, you just see it. When you prophesy, it just comes on you. However, the power gifts—miracles, healings, and faith—require a deeper understanding to employ them successfully. Each operates not only as a Holy Spirit gift but also on another level. Often, people don't understand the distinction between (1) faith (sometimes called simple faith) and the gift of faith, (2) a miracle and the gift of working of miracles, and (3) a healing and the gifts of healings, which is even listed plurally.

Holy Spirit's gifts differ from their counterparts because with regular faith, miracles, and healings, you pray and apply tools—Scripture, fasting, prayer. However, we all know people who've been prayed for but have gone away empty-handed without their healing. When someone comes for a healing, you need to understand the prayer process for the answer to come. However, praying by using your faith process isn't the only way to receive that answer. Another level comes as Holy Spirit's gifts become part of the equation. With the gifts of faith, miracles, and healings, Holy Spirit deposits an extra certainty in you that the work is done, and that seals the answer. Also, when the healing you're seeking is revealed through other gifts, that healing or miracle occurs as a natural consequence of that revelation. When that gift couples with other gifts like words of knowledge, healing is natural, sure, and even simple. Holy Spirit creates that answer, and we don't have to use our faith formula.

Partnership

Therefore, in my experience, automatic healings occur when Holy Spirit partners this healing gift with other gifts. As we said before, separating revelation and speaking gifts from power gifts is difficult because gifts work in tandem with one another. When I pray for people, healings and miracles come routinely after a revelation or prophetic word. When the Spirit gets involved and utilizes other gifts, He brings that answer by giving a rhema about the need. Then we see the promise's manifestation as that rhema allows us to "be diligent to enter that rest" (Heb. 4:11). We diligently say what God's spoken and how to bring healing. Then we rest, knowing it's done.

Hundreds of times, God's given Wade, another person, or me a word of knowledge. When that word comes, an anointing is present for whatever God revealed. I compare this pairing of words of knowledge with the healing gift to the man trying to get into the pool of Bethesda (see John 5:4). The angel is stirring the water right then; if we take advantage, healing will surely happen. Because of the massive numbers of healings and miracles we've seen in conjunction with words of knowledge, Wade and I, as well as others who attend our meetings, often say with confidence, "What He reveals, He heals." *Done deal!*

Holy Spirit seals the healing through this gift in other ways too; when that happens, healing also occurs. Once on Facebook, I asked for prayer for a list of Christian women who couldn't conceive. One of my former students saw that and asked me to add her name. A few weeks later, as I mentioned her in prayer a knowing settled over me that whether she was pregnant right then or in the future, that prayer had already been answered. I sent her a message, and she responded that she was glad I'd contacted her because she needed encouragement that day. She and her husband had become so disheartened they were contemplating in-vitro fertilization. Soon, she messaged me that a test came back positive, and she now has a baby girl. When Holy Spirit puts that knowing, that gift of faith, in us, it has happened or will happen. Healing, deliverance, even pregnancies must occur. *Done deal!*

When God reveals a word of knowledge followed by speaking or power gifts, situations change. It just happens. Through the years of witnessing it, I've grown to understand the it's-gonna-be-done aspect of receiving God's words. Answers come by our hearing then obeying what God has shown. Whether our part is just praying or doing an action, obedience is crucial.

Other Holy Spirit Helps

Holy Spirit uses other tools to partner with healing. Sometimes He gives special anointings to ministries for a certain malady. Wade and I have experienced many occurrences of particular healings, so we have specific faith for those—legs lengthened, backs healed, pregnancies occurring. We've also seen that when people have been healed from an affliction, they often possess an anointing to help others because freely they've received, so they pass it along (see Matt. 10:8). Years ago in Arizona, I had a shingles outbreak on my leg. Annabelle, a lovely lady, had been healed from that years before. She prayed, and I slowly saw blisters dry up. The healing's completion took time, but they didn't return.

Prophetic actions and travail will be further explored in another section. Briefly, prophetic actions are when Holy Spirit gives direction for something the seeker should do to bring the answer. Naaman was healed by dipping in the Jordan (see 2 Kings 5:1-19), and the Shunammite woman's son was raised from the dead as Elisha laid his body on top of the boy (see 2 Kings 4:35). These actions produce results because someone heard, obeyed, and acted; then deliverance came. Travail, another amazing tool, is described in the Bible as a woman giving birth (see John 16:21), its pangs producing whatever you're praying for. Sometimes, prayers feel like they're ineffectively trying to pierce a wall of sickness, hardship, or other afflictions. Travail is a strong breakthrough anointing to shatter that wall. It's not pretty—loud, boisterous sobs so hard the body often shakes. However, when I need an answer, I seek out those weird, loud travailers to bring breakthrough. *Done deal!*

A glorious way Holy Spirit's gifts bring healing is by going into God's presence, usually through worship. We've learned that when we bask there, Kingdom manifestations occur. We've seen the glory manifest many ways—miracles, a blanket of peace, fog, angelic feathers, and other wonders. Other ministries have experienced Holy Spirit's presence as rain in the middle of the church or fire so powerful that people outside have called the fire department. Other places have received manna and jewels. I've heard those manifestations described as God's kisses. I like that. He told Elijah He'd reserved seven thousand "whose knees have not bowed to Baal, and every mouth that has not kissed him" (1 Kings 19:18). The word for kiss is *nashaq*, "to kiss, lit. or fig—[but also] to equip with weapons."[1] As we kiss God and He kisses us in worship, He arms us with weapons we'll need for the raging battle. Going into His glory equips us to assure victory, even with a healing.

Worship is a vital aspect of warfare. In conjunction with worship, God attacks our enemy with "swinging and menacing arms" (Isa. 30:32 AMPC). Don't you love the picture of the Lord's "menacing arms" knocking down everything in our path—cancer, marital problems, financial woes? Manifestations, though, are for more than just signs and wonders. In His presence we gain intimacy. Sometimes, we sit silently and soak or wait on the Lord and let Him do whatever He desires. He replenishes us physically and spiritually so we then have substance to give out, or He brings clarity to life's situations. His presence generates what's needed because we observe the key—to be with Him. The rest comes as a bonus. *Done deal!*

A Process

Healings differ from miracles because they occur over time. I've heard some say Jesus' healings never were a process but rather immediate miracles. Mark addresses that. In Bethsaida, people brought Jesus a blind man to heal. He took the man by the hand and went out of town. Then, He spat on the man's eyes, laid hands upon Him, and asked what he saw. The man's response was, "I see men like trees, walking" (Mark 8:24). Jesus laid hands upon him and prayed once again; he was completely healed. This story tells me that sometimes our answer doesn't come when we first pray. I remember services as a child when we prayed intensely and waited on the Lord for one person until breakthrough came. God doesn't get in a hurry, and neither should we as we pray. He determines who needs our intercession, when, and how long it should take.

The issue for many in our services, though, is that we're so used to the miraculous that we expect it and don't want to wait. After prayer, we'll ask if pain is gone. If people say, "It's better," we usually pray for them to be whole, not partially healed. Frequently, they're healed totally. However, even with supernatural healings, nature often has work to do. Jesus explained that in a parable (see Mark 4:26-29). When a piece of corn is sowed into the ground, growth starts at that point. However, time's required before evidence of a harvest—a sprout grows into a stalk that bears an ear of corn, which still needs time to ripen. Faith says even in the incipient phases, growth has begun despite contrary evidence. Through faith we don't waver in knowing the final reaping will happen. If at any time you dig it up with words of fear or unbelief, you start all over because that disturbs the natural process.

I saw that wondrous process as I watched the healing of a woman I don't even know. I'd become acquainted with a local flea market vendor. When he bought one of my Gates books for his wife, crippled with a debilitating syndrome, I put her on our prayer list then took him a prayer cloth. When I'd see him, he'd report that she was doing better. Then concrete improvements came—she could move her thumb, then her fingers, then her legs. One day, when I hadn't seen him for several weeks, as I walked toward his booth, he caught my eye, smiled enormously, and waved boisterously. I knew something wonderful had happened. He walked toward me rapidly and proclaimed his wife was no longer in a wheelchair but able to get around using a walker.

He told me, "She said, 'Throw that wheelchair away 'cause I'm never gonna use it again!'" They're thrilled that God had chosen a chance encounter at the flea market to bring them a gift. It wasn't the *boom* healing we would have liked, but she continues to improve as God brings the seed that was planted and watered into manifestation.

Symptoms

Although healing is done and completion takes time to occur, in the meantime you may still deal with symptoms. Claiming to be healed is hard when you hurt; therefore, many give up and say they weren't healed when actually they're just experiencing residual symptoms. Sometimes, even when we pray again and they get better, people still feel symptoms. I often tell them to remember the process of the corn. Whether even minor improvements come today or tomorrow, God has begun the work. Also, although you become symptom-free after the prayer, symptoms sometimes may come back later because the enemy wants to steal that miracle. Jonah calls those symptoms "lying vanities" (see Jonah 2:8 KJV) because satan wants to convince you the sickness has returned when actually you're still healed. You're just experiencing symptoms.

Just out of college, I suffered with a common ailment for me—canker sores. In the summer, when I drank Cokes and ate fresh tomatoes from the garden, sores would get so bad I could barely talk—quite an impediment for a brand-new high school teacher. My Sunday-school teacher prayed for me then told me to rebuke the symptoms if sores didn't leave right away. I did, and for two weeks symptoms were still there. And they hurt! I didn't give up, though. I knew that prayer had touched heaven and I was healed. Every day, I claimed healing despite what I felt like; but after they dried up, I've never had them again. God's healing was complete and has been for over forty years. Symptoms aren't the disease, so you can be healed and still feel sick. During the interim, don't allow satan to turn a victory into a defeat.

Covenants of Healing

As an operator in the gifts, knowing Holy Spirit brings about healings through various weapons is liberating. He does the work for us, through us. So what happens if Holy Spirit isn't activated? Can healing still occur? Absolutely! Healing is our heritage. David said to "Bless the Lord…and forget not all His benefits: who forgives all your iniquities, who heals all your diseases" (Ps. 103:2-3). Because we're His, we have certain "benefits"—forgiveness from sin *plus* healing. How awesome is that! Just like the benefits package we receive from that new job, joining God's family gives us healing in our package. We need to trust that our answer will happen because we have a healing promise in three ways.

First, we have a healing covenant. God showed Himself as Healer on the wilderness journey. In Exodus 15, the Hebrews made their way across the desert, and, once again, they were without water for three days. Now I know their complaining was irritating; but in reality, this situation was critical. According to the US Forest Service training manual, going three days without water is a serious threat to a human's survival,[2] especially in hot climates. In other words, their circumstance was dire; then they came to the waters of Marah. Excitement soon died as they realized those waters were poisoned.

However, God used this wilderness experience to reveal Himself on another level—their Healer. He said:

If you diligently heed the voice of the Lord your God and do what is right in His sight, give ear to His commandments and keep all His statutes, I will put none of the diseases on you which I have brought on the Egyptians. For I am the Lord who heals you (Exodus 15:26).

From then on, He became Jehovah Ropheka, "the Lord who heals." This story speaks on many levels about this Healer we all need to know at some point. At times healing is simple—our baby's ear infection, an upset stomach, a hurting finger. However, often we come to Jehovah Ropheka for healing so grim we have no other hope. Doctors say cancer has spread, and we can count life expectancy in weeks. Our child is diagnosed with Parkinson's or lupus, which will only get worse. A friend has AIDS. Those are bitter-water experiences at Marah, where the desert of infirmity will prevail if Jehovah Ropheka doesn't intervene. That's when knowing covenant rights and responsibilities will bring about our dear Father's promise.

Our second healing covenant was through Jesus. Isaiah gave the promise of Healer: "He was wounded for our transgressions, He was bruised for our iniquities; the chastisement for our peace was upon Him, and by His stripes we are healed" (Isa. 53:5). Jesus was destined for the cross but had to endure much—one friend's betrayal, another's denial, His disciples' apathy, and a vicious scourging that may have cost His life. He could have avoided it all, but He didn't. He was His Father's Son, and like His Dad, said, "I'm gonna let My people know Me as a Healer." He took stripes with one purpose—our healing—big, little, and everything in between. It's we, not He, who limit His ability. Even before Holy Spirit came, disciples were healing in Jesus' name (see Matt. 10:1). Now we can call on that name and appropriate those stripes Isaiah foretold. When Peter quoted Isaiah, he said by Jesus' stripes we "were healed" (1 Pet. 2:24). As Jesus fulfilled that prophecy, He put our healing in the past tense. *Done deal!* Now we can appropriate healing where it's needed because He came not only for sins, but to heal too (see Matt. 9:5). It's part of our covenant promises.

The final healing covenant is through Holy Spirit and operation of the gifts. Holy Spirit brings victory by His character and provides healing weapons. Words of knowledge and wisdom just make it happen. Prophetic words and actions bring healing with rhemas that give revelation. When Jesus promised another Comforter (see John 14:16), He used the word *parakletos*, an "intercessor, consoler—advocate, comforter,"[3] Holy Spirit. His use of *another* was the word *allos*, meaning "one besides, another of the same kind."[4] They're all teaming up on our behalf. Holy Spirit partners with Jesus to heal and deliver with *exousia* and *dunamis* power strong enough to move mountains. The Father, Son, and Holy Spirit—a powerful, healing heritage that belongs to all. God's character revealed healing. Jesus brought exousia power with the authority of His name. Then He took healing stripes and gave His life for our salvation and healing. Holy Spirit dwells within His people and gives power to move heaven and earth. The Godhead all have healing aspects of their characters and can make that happen. That's a prescription a typical doctor can't order.

His Word

Many ignore an amazing healing tool—God's Word through which you can find a promise to bring that elusive healing into reality. His Word is sharper than a surgeon's knife and can cut into a man's spirit (see Heb. 4:12). He says, "If you abide in My word, you are My disciples indeed. And you shall know the truth, and the truth shall make you free" (John 8:31-32). Setting up residence in His Word brings freedom, even from sickness. His Word is truth that allows you to step beyond earthly circumstances and into healing. When God speaks into your spirit that a Scripture is for this situation, it becomes your rhema to hold on to. Can you find a promise that speaks to you?

- "He sent His word and healed them, and delivered them from their destructions" (Ps 107:20).
- "Worship the Lord your God, and his blessing will be on your food and water. I will take away sickness from among you" (Exod. 23:25 NIV).
- He desires that we "may prosper in all things and be in health, just as [our] soul prospers" (3 John 1:2).
- "O Lord my God, I cried out to You, and You healed me" (Ps. 30:2).
- We "shall not die, but live, and declare the works of the Lord" (Ps. 118:17).

How could you possibly speak those Scriptures without your healing heritage getting into your spirit and resulting in an answer? Isaiah says that any word going from your mouth doesn't come back void, so those words *must* apply to healing (see Isa. 55:11). When you find your rhema, Holy Spirit's giving a promise, and God's Word doesn't lie. *Done deal!*

Our Words

You should be aware not only of the power of God's Word but also of your own words. Your words determine how you receive, and you then speak your future. When Joshua marched around Jericho (see Josh. 2), those walls represented a breakthrough—physical, spiritual, emotional, anything. He told his people that no one was to speak during any of those first twelve trips around the walls. Why? I'm sure others wondered what craziness Joshua had dragged them into, but God had a reason. Speaking doom could counteract God's purpose for breakthrough. Often, you receive healing then negate it by your words. Once your mouth declares your healing didn't happen, you're officially sick again. You can accept its return, or you can keep your healing. You should say, "In the name of Jesus, I'm healed, and I'm not giving that back." Your words are a wonderful weapon or a terrible enemy for healing.

I've sometimes prayed for someone and felt power go into him/her. I knew, however, healing wouldn't happen when I finished praying and that person spoke words laden with unbelief. I once heard a speaker tell about a service where God moved for a lady in depression's throes. She was touched; even her countenance changed. Later, the woman testified she felt like a different person—until the service's end. When walking out, as she shook hands with the pastor, the whine returned as she said, "Pastor, pray for me. That old depression has me." It did have her once those words left her mouth! The lady who related this story said she could see that spirit settle back onto the woman. Mouths should declare victory rather than defeat, faith instead of fear. You can be prayed for by every anointed preacher who comes along, but your part is believing and watching your words—what you say and how you say it. They literally hold the power of life and death, sickness and healing over you.

WWJD

If you want to know how healing works, look at Jesus, who healed, healed, and then healed some more. Those healings often happened through prophetic actions—mud on the eyes (see John 9:11), instructing a man to take up his bed (see John 5:8), spitting on His fingers and touching a man's tongue (see Mark 7:33).

And Jesus went about all Galilee, teaching in their synagogues, preaching the gospel of the kingdom, and healing all kinds of sickness and all kinds of disease among the people. Then His fame went throughout all Syria; and they brought to Him all sick people who were afflicted with various diseases and torments, and those who were demon-possessed, epileptics, and paralytics; and He healed them (Matthew 4:23-24).

"And He healed them." Healing was Jesus' character. When we utilize God's amazing gifts of healings, people seek us out. With Jesus as our example, we'll see our gift not as a way to be esteemed but rather as an opportunity to serve. When throngs bombarded Jesus, He went to the sea and prepared an escape route in case the massive crowd crushed Him, "For He [had] healed many, so that as many as had afflictions pressed about Him to touch Him" (Mark 3:10). That word for *healed* is *therapeuo*, "to wait upon menially…to adore (God), or (spec.) to relieve (of disease)—cure, heal, worship."[5] Think of that meaning! Jesus healed because He served all who came, just like a servant charged with any job. This healing gift humbles us as servants then gives Him glory, like every other job we do for God. When we become servants like Jesus, healing is our character, too.

Faith and Desperation

The Bible is clear about faith's role in healing:

Is anyone among you sick? Let him call for the elders of the church, and let them pray over him, anointing him with oil in the name of the Lord. And the prayer of faith will save the sick, and the Lord will raise him up. And if he has committed sins, he will be forgiven. Confess your trespasses to one another, and pray for one another, that you may be healed. The effective, fervent prayer of a righteous man avails much (James 5:14-16).

Faith brings results, and so does desperation. I love the story of the woman who approached Jesus for her child to be delivered from demonic possession. At first, He ignored her then said healing was the children's bread (see Matt. 15:16). Though Jesus told the heathen woman that healing was for His people, she persisted and broke through (see Matt. 15). He said, "'O woman, great is your faith! Let it be to you as you desire.' And her daughter was healed from that very hour" (Matt. 15:28). Her faith brought her daughter's healing because she saw the Healer and pressed in. God doesn't heal in response to fear but rather to faith and desperation, just like with this woman.

Other scriptural answers came after someone reached the point of desperation. When the Shunammite woman's child died, she raced to Elisha; her "soul was in distress" (2 Kings 4:27). Hannah cried in the temple, desperately sought God, and "wept in anguish" (1 Sam. 1:10). God responded and rewarded the Shunammite woman's "distress" with her son's resurrection and Hannah's "anguish" with a baby who became Israel's greatest prophet and judge. After Isaiah revealed that Hezekiah would die from his illness, Hezekiah desperately sought God. As a result, God said, "I have heard your prayer, I have seen your tears; surely I will heal you" (2 Kings 20:5). After Isaiah spoke this and performed the prophetic action of putting figs on Hezekiah's boil, God gave him fifteen more years. Our Father looks at faith and hopelessness and responds when we pour ourselves out to Him. Desperation brings healing into our realm because we have no hope except to give it to Him and believe.

In the first six or so months of my twins' lives, we made numerous trips to the pediatrician, usually for ear infections. That spring day, Jill held her ear, ran a fever, and showed signs that, once again, I'd be dealing with another infection. I was desperate. Every day, I did all that exhausted every new mother—twice. I had little sleep with nightly feedings and changings, working full time, then taking many trips on that windy country road to the doctor's office. I couldn't take anymore. That afternoon, sitting on the corner of the bed in the back upstairs bedroom of our farmhouse, I cried out in desperation.

"I need help!" I sobbed. "I don't want her sick again, and I'm beyond what I can physically do. Please heal my Jilly." As I held her closer, pouring out my heart to Him, the curtains at the open window fluttered toward me, but no breeze blew outside. An anointing came in stronger than I'd ever felt. As the presence hovered over Jill and me, I knew she was being healed. She immediately responded—her fever broke and her whimpering stopped. She opened her eyes, looked contentedly at me, snuggled against me, and fell into a peaceful sleep—healed. She never had another ear infection until high school when she was on the swim team. Jennifer, however, whom I didn't cover with my prayers, had many. God responded that day and others to my desperation.

Conclusion

I've seen people disappointed because they came for healing that didn't happen. However, despite what our eyes and bodies perceive, we should see eternal truths, not temporary problems like ear infections and canker sores (see 2 Cor. 4:18). If we look through faith's eyes, we see ourselves and others healed. Remember when Jesus scolded disciples for their lack of faith then told them many deliverances come with prayer and fasting (see Matt. 17:21)? We do all we know to get healing—prayer, travail, prophetic actions, Scriptures, fasting. Then we stand on His word and wait for our answer (see Eph. 6:13-14). If we listen to Holy Spirit, many things make a difference. Our prayers open pathways for God to answer, including healings. We can look to other natural sources, but the Spirit who lives in us brings Spirit results (see Rom. 8:9-11). As Holy Spirit quickens His plan, we find victory as we listen, obey, and believe. How simple, yet profound! The key is, "If you seek Him, He will be found by you" (1 Chron. 28:9). When we find Him and know His heart, *done deal!*

PROPHETIC ACTIONS

Wade

In combat, battle plans rarely transpire as designed. Instantaneous tactical reactions to combat situations are essential to assure victory. Every battle is unique regarding terrain, enemy position, firepower, and strategic options. Frequently, indirect artillery fire support is required to rout enemy positions. This is much like prophetic proclamations in the midst of spiritual warfare. Often, natural warfare requires bold maneuvering and spur-of-the-moment decision-making to overcome enemy resistance. Prophetic action is the spiritual counterpart to battlefield tactics to outmaneuver the enemy. Prophetic actions require instantaneous obedience to Holy Spirit's prompting and direction for destroying enemy strongholds and freeing people from enemy oppression.

How They Work

Revelation 19:10 states, "For the testimony of Jesus is the spirit of prophecy." The spirit of prophecy, Jesus' testimony, is that He did only what He saw the Father doing and spoke only what He heard the Father saying (see John 5:19-21). Jesus gave His disciples (us) the mandate and anointing to minister in the authority of His name and Holy Spirit's power. Paul confirmed this: "For our gospel did not come to you in word only, but also in power, and in the Holy Spirit and in much assurance" (1 Thess. 1:5). The spirit of prophecy is the testimony of Jesus Christ. I refer to His spirit of prophecy as "prophetic action."

Gifts of healings and working of miracles often manifest through prophetic actions. I describe them as this—words that act and actions that speak. For example, once when ministering in a healing line, Holy Spirit prompted me to tell a woman whose body was twisted from severe rheumatoid arthritis, "You should forgive him—he's been dead thirty years!" I obeyed, spoke, and immediately ministered to the next person. That prophetic instruction began to take effect. As I was ministering down the prayer line, I heard audible popping sounds and looked back to witness gnarled, crooked joints miraculously straightened by Holy Spirit's power. Soon she was running and jumping through the church as Holy Spirit delivered and healed her. She looked like a different person, having been set free from effects of unforgiveness, bitterness, and self-rejection that had manifested in her body. That's prophetic action's power.

At times Holy Spirit will impress me to activate a prophetic word He's given. This may involve laying on of hands or instructing the person to act on the word by moving and doing something he/ she couldn't do before because of pain or limited range of motion. This prophetic action causes the word to be established, resulting in deliverance, healings, and miracles. Holy Spirit once impressed me to speak to a man that he would receive a million-dollar idea. He was an independent trucker experiencing such financial hardship that his wife was having yard sales to make house and truck payments. The Spirit told me to have him hold his hands in front of him, palms up, and activate this word by slapping his hands. The stinging effect of that action was what broke off the spirit of poverty oppressing his family. Within a year, he had hauling contracts for over a million dollars. He's still prospering even in these hard times when other independent truckers have gone out of business.

Jesus ministered through prophetic actions. If we want the same results He had (and promised we'd do), we must do what He did (see John 14:12-14). These same and greater works will result from prophetic action—speaking and doing what Holy Spirit authors. Prophetic actions have become second nature to Connie and me. We expect Holy Spirit to reveal words of knowledge and the method by which He desires to heal, restore, or create His will.

Prophetic actions are often the precursor to Holy Spirit's works of power. Robert, legally blind, was brought into a Sunday evening service. During ministry, he was helped to the front for prayer and was slain in the Spirit as I prayed. While lying on the floor, Herb was led by Holy Spirit to come forward, kneel beside Robert, and blow on his eyes. After several minutes, he regained consciousness, opened his eyes, and exclaimed, "I see the rafters!" Holy Spirit had healed his blindness through simple obedience and the prophetic action of blowing on his eyes. Awesome!

Biblical Examples

Throughout Scripture, prophetic actions resulted in amazing works of power. For example, Moses used his rod to perform many miracles. In Exodus 14, he stretched it out over the Red Sea and waters divided. In Exodus 17:6, he struck the rock and water gushed forth. In Exodus 17:8-16, as Amalek battled with Israel in Rephidim, he stood on a hill overlooking the battlefield. As he raised his rod, Israel prevailed against Amalek; when he tired and let his rod down, Amalek prevailed. Israel gained victory because Aaron and Hur stood beside Moses and held up his hands with the rod over the battlefield. These were powerful prophetic actions.

In Second Samuel 6:12-23, David, along with the Levites, brought the Ark of the Covenant back to Jerusalem. He took six steps then offered a sacrifice to the Lord. Six represents the number of man. David's prophetic action indicated he'd come to an end of himself and his own ability as he presented himself a sacrifice to God. David was acting out this vicarious sacrificial offering in the bloody trip with the Ark from Obed-Edom's house to Mt. Zion in Jerusalem. Paul wrote of sacrifice:

I beseech you therefore, brethren, by the mercies of God, that you present your bodies a living sacrifice, holy, acceptable to God, which is your reasonable service. And do not be conformed to this world, but be transformed by the renewing of your mind, that you may prove what is that good and acceptable and perfect will of God (Romans 12:1-2).

Another example of prophetic action is in Second Kings 13:14-19. Elisha was old and about to die. King Joash visited the prophet, who told him to take a bow and shoot an arrow out the east window. The prophet put his hands on the king's hands as he released it. This prophetic action was an arrow of deliverance from Syria. Elisha then told Joash to take arrows and strike the ground. When he struck only three times and stopped, the prophet became angry and said he should have struck the ground five or six times, for Joash would have victory over the Syrians only three times. Through prophetic action, Joash was assured of victory; by limiting his action, he also limited God's deliverance from Israel's enemies. This tells me when God says to strike the ground, we should keep pounding until He says stop! Prophetic actions not only are precursors to the working of miracles; they also often determine destiny.

Boomerang Effect

John's revelation provides a unique portrait of prophetic action, which I call the boomerang effect. Most know the boomerang as a curved stick used by Australian aborigines to distract prey as they throw it and it returns to them. Our prophetic actions are like spiritual boomerangs we release into the Spirit realm, which return to earth with Kingdom manifestations.

Revelation 5:8 is a panoramic visionary scene unfolding in heaven as four living creatures and twenty-four elders fall before the Lamb. Each holds a golden bowl full of incense, which are saints' prayers. In Revelation 8:3-5, an angel stands with a golden censer filled with incense offered with saints' prayers before the throne.

Smoke from the incense ascends before God from the angel's hand. Then the angel fills the censer with fire and throws it to earth. The results are noises, thunder, lightning, and earthquakes. Our prayers and prophetic actions fill the golden bowls of heaven with heaven's response resulting in miracle manifestations on earth.

Perhaps the most descriptive example of the boomerang effect is in Daniel 10:1-13. Daniel had been fasting and praying for twenty-one days when an angel appeared to him, saying:

> *Do not fear, Daniel, for from the first day that you set your heart to understand, and to humble yourself before your God, your words were heard; and I have come because of your words. But the prince of the kingdom of Persia withstood me twenty-one days; and behold, Michael, one of the chief princes, came to help me, for I had been left alone there with the kings of Persia* (Daniel 10:12-13).

What do you think would have happened if Daniel had stopped his prayer and fasting before the twenty-one days ended? Would there have been enough spiritual substance from Daniel's prayers to fill heavenly golden bowls for spiritual breakthrough on earth? My opinion is that twenty-one days of prophetic action of Daniel's fasting and prayer created spiritual substance for the archangel Michael to break through the ruling demon over Persia. As Daniel threw out that boomerang of fasting and praying, it came back as answered prayer and an angelic visitation.

Conclusion

God once gave Connie a prophetic action to have everyone pin money to the clothes of a lady who wanted to step into ministry but was hindered by financial problems, limited speaking opportunities, and an unsupportive husband. As we pinned money to her, we gathered around and prayed. Her ministry changed immediately. Beginning that week, money came from several sources. Since then, she's been asked to speak many times, God's provided money, and her husband went with her on ministry trips. God took a seemingly impossible situation and changed it. Prophetic action is a dynamic weapon in spiritual warfare.

Consider Paul and Silas—beaten, wounded, and placed in stocks in the stinking prison's belly. As they sang praises and worshiped God at midnight, heaven responded to their prophetic action with an earthquake, setting other prisoners free and resulting in multiple salvations (see Acts 16:16-34). Prophetic actions accomplish God's work in every situation. Sometimes, Holy Spirit prompts you to do something as simple as clap, shout, stomp, smile, or give a word of encouragement. When that happens, you've released a spiritual substance into the heavenly realm to be multiplied then released back to earth's environment. You've begun your journey in prophetic actions. Being obedient in little things qualifies you for promotion to bigger assignments. Without obedience, you impede His plans and purposes in earth, for we're the ones with dominion (see Gen. 1:26). We're heaven's ambassadors on earth and His earthly royal priesthood (see 2 Cor. 5:20; 1 Pet. 2:9). Let's do our part—listen, hear, and obey—then see His miraculous, wonder-working power manifested.

WORKING OF MIRACLES

Wade

It has been several decades since I served in Vietnam as a military advisor. Back then, science fiction didn't come close to what exists today. I'm amazed at weaponry's technological advancement, intelligence-gathering capability, and power available. The working of miracles is similar. Many believers have never seen or even imagined Holy Spirit's wonder-working power to create or instantaneously heal the impossible. We've only scratched the surface of possibilities through Holy Spirit's weapon of the working of miracles!

Janie arrived a few minutes early to our Times of Refreshing meeting. She almost didn't come because of severe back pain. Connie positioned her on a chair and held her extended legs. One was decidedly shorter. I wandered over, stood behind her chair, and put my hands on her shoulders. We commanded her back and legs to come into alignment and any obstructions corrected. Then something happened. Janie's legs, still in Connie's hands, moved discernibly. The obvious difference in length from before was just as obviously corrected as one of the legs literally slid toward Connie.

Janie's eyes grew wide. She said, "I just felt something pop and twist in my hip joint and heat flow through my body." Connie released her grip on Janie's legs, told her to stand, and asked her to do something she couldn't do before.

As she moved from side to side, she shook her head and said, "No pain. Pain's gone." She told us that twenty-one years earlier, while she'd been pregnant, doctors discovered a hip condition she'd had since birth. She'd lived with pain, which had become excruciating as her daughter's birth had repositioned her hip and affected her lower back. She moved about, then jumped and danced for joy. The long-time pain was gone. Her excitement was contagious, and others who'd gathered around rejoiced with her.

She grabbed Connie. "That's a miracle! It's a miracle!" she blurted.

Connie said, "Janie, we always have miracles in our services."

She didn't miss a beat as she replied, "Yeah, I know. But this one was for me!" We can witness miracles; but when they happen to us, we never forget God's great power and love. By the way, that's a good way to start a meeting!

Power

As believers operating in the kingdom principle of dominion (see Gen. 1:26), we have both Jesus' delegated authority and Holy Spirit's power to operate in the working of miracles. Knowing we have the capacity to do greater works than Jesus is the first step in working of miracles (see John 14:12). Believers must recognize they're dual-realm creations with authority both on earth and the spirit realm through Holy Spirit. After receiving revelation about how to proceed for a miracle, you mustn't allow your carnal mind to analyze His instructions. When you don't immediately act on His word, the miracle will likely not occur because it will make no logical sense. Logic is the culprit that stops the miracle process. Romans 8:6-7 states the "carnal mind" is in bitter opposition with God and "to be carnally minded is death, but to be spiritually minded is life and peace" (Rom. 8:6). As new creations, all things (divine revelation and works of power) are possible to them who believe (see Mark 9:23).

Once while ministering outdoors in Bowie, Arizona, Connie had a word of knowledge about a growth under someone's arm. A lady there said she'd already undergone a mastectomy, and her doctor had told her cancer had returned with a sizable tumor beneath her arm.

We knew what God reveals, He's there to heal. Connie laid hands on her and released power into her body. The lady was slain in the Spirit and fell to the gravel. Later, when she went to the doctor, the tumor had disappeared! Our responsibility in the working of miracles is to believe and instantly obey when Holy Spirit speaks. Then the Spirit's power takes over and manifests miracles.

Creative Miracles

The working of miracles operates through God's Kingdom principles with the natural realm complying. Romans 8:19-22 explains that creation groans and labors with birth pangs to be delivered from its cursed condition. Creation longs to cooperate with believers who understand and exercise authority and dominion. Working of miracles occurs through Kingdom principles releasing resurrection power through existing substance, just as Jesus demonstrated. Miracles are acts of power not just employing existing substance but also "like substance."

Study scriptural miracles, and ask Holy Spirit to reveal the truth behind every one. When the ax head fell in the river, Elisha cut off a stick that would float and threw it into the water, causing the iron ax head to float (see 2 Kings 6:5-7). Jesus turned one type of liquid substance (water) into another type of liquid substance (wine) (see John 2:6-9). When Jesus spoke His word (invisible, *pneuma*), it calmed the wind (invisible) that was influencing the waves. When He multiplied bread and fishes, He used a little to produce a lot; disciples distributed bread and fish that multiplied in their hands (see Matt. 14:17-21; 15:32-38). In John 9:6, Jesus created eyeballs by spitting on clay and forming it to fit into the man's eye sockets. Adam was formed from dust (see Gen. 2:7). Understanding how this concept works is easy once you visualize it and cooperate with Holy Spirit. By emulating what Father spoke and did, the creative power of Jesus' spoken words and prophetic actions brought about miracle-working results, just as they will for us.

As we've said before, healings are progressive while miracles happen instantaneously, defying natural limitations of time and space. Scripture's full of creative miracle examples—fertility imparted into Abraham and Sarah to birth Isaac, plagues of Egypt, parting of the Red Sea, manna from heaven, limitless supply of meal and oil, supernatural oil to pay off a creditor, the dead resurrected, battlefield victories, and many others. Jesus often used creative miracles. All these acts of power have been recorded as lessons about how miracles operate. If this isn't true, then why would the working of miracles be included as one of the gifts of Holy Spirit? It's up to us to discover the lessons of the miracles!

I've been asked to pray for those who lost organ function and have nothing remaining to be healed. Instead of praying for healing, a creative miracle is required to replace affected organs. Once, I prayed for a creative miracle of new lungs for a man in intensive care on a ventilator. Holy Spirit moved; he was out of the hospital the next day. We often pray for creative miracles for dire physical, financial, and relational situations and see God's mighty, wonder-working power. When we seek His wisdom, Holy Spirit leads in how to pray, to declare God's word, and to act to bring about His manifestations. Once we receive His wisdom, we can have absolute confidence in His results. That's how uncomplicated and accessible faith is for working of miracles.

Faith's Part

The gift of faith operates in tandem with the working of miracles. Holy Spirit deposits faith for miracles within those who believe and expect miracles to manifest. Faith's the divine force that substantiates our white-hot expectation (hope) and is the title deed to our miracle. We get what we expect, like a thermostat where we dial in the desired temperature, and the power of an air conditioner or furnace (Holy Spirit) works to bring manifestation. Most of us expect too little from God. He's much bigger than our expectations, so we should anticipate more—big things like national revival, reformation, and miracles.

When Connie and I minister, we expect the Spirit to reveal His secrets and do works of power. He never disappoints! We've witnessed blinded eyes see, deaf ears hear, tumors disappear, legs grow out, and on and on. It has little to do with us—it's applying expectation with willingness and instant obedience. Our responsibility is to do what He says; the results are Holy Spirit's job. That takes the pressure off us! I've heard other ministers say, "What if they don't get healed? How will that make me look?" Let's face it. We couldn't heal a gnat of a headache by ourselves! All Holy Spirit needs is our availability, willingness, and obedience for miracles to manifest.

An excellent example of how faith resulted in miracles was an elderly woman named Emma Stroupe, who has since gone to be with God. She and her husband were missionaries and evangelists until he died; then she ventured out on her own. Nothing stopped her! She once said that when she was in a North Carolina seminary, the dean came into an assembly one afternoon and asked, "Who here believes God can raise the dead?" All raised their hands. He then asked, "Who believes you can raise the dead through God's power?" Young Emma and another girl raised their hands and were led to where the school's caretaker had just died. Those girls entered the house; about an hour later, all three walked out. The caretaker had been raised through the gift of faith and God's miracle-working power as those two girls believed He would.

Sister Stroupe was responsible for building many churches in the Philippines; Haiti; and, as she called it, "Africar." She lived on a meager social security check and expected God to provide. He supernaturally supplied thousands of dollars to build churches and supply ministry resources in remote areas of the world where most wouldn't dare to go. Her faith didn't just cover financial needs, though. She told many stories of God's miracle-working power and never differentiated between a huge or small miracle. To her, slapping the back of a lady suffering with cancer and seeing her instantly healed was the same as asking the Lord to give her a candy bar then turning the corner to find a fully wrapped Snickers bar on the sidewalk. When we pastored, Sister Stroupe would often come to our services. I'd seat her in front to minister to those needing healings and miracles. She'd follow the Spirit's leading in every case—sometimes hitting them with her cane. Oh and by the way, they'd get healed! When I think of someone expecting, believing God, and instantly obeying Him, Sister Stroupe comes to mind.

Hands-On Learning

As mentioned earlier, the working of miracles is also designed to be a spiritual classroom to gain understanding of God's heart and ways. One key to spiritual maturity is to understand everything done through Holy Spirit's power has multilayered purpose. Of course, the miracle's benefits are obvious to those receiving the miracle, but those through whom the miracle comes are also beneficiaries. Operating in the working of miracles and gifts of healings is humbling. One quickly recognizes these gifts are not about him/her—to make a name or get in the spotlight of human acclaim. We've all seen those with self-promoting motives fall from their manmade platforms. Don't allow God's miracles to lose their intended eternal effectiveness in your life. They're much bigger and far more important than that marvelous one-time event.

As previously mentioned, Holy Spirit's weapons operate in conjunction one with another. For example, revelation (rhema) comes from our Commander with the authority (exousia) and power (dunamis) to create the miraculous and usher in Kingdom manifestations. In fact, when God speaks, that rhema is already "framed" (see Heb. 11:3), established, and completed in the eternal Spirit realm. Rhema is the transporter of the gift of faith imparted into a believer's spirit. Hearing the word brings supernatural power (dunamis) contained within the rhema to accomplish the revelation's purpose (see Rom. 10:17). The believer's power partnership with Holy Spirit is in proportion to the degree the mind is renewed to prove God's will (see Rom. 12:2). The believer, armed with Holy Spirit's rhema containing faith (authority and power) intercedes through prophetic action. Simple obedience to the Spirit's leading results in Kingdom manifestations of healings, miracles, signs, and wonders.

Just as an expert hunter tracks his prey and knows signs of its presence, so also we're to become aware of the Spirit's subtle signals and teaching moments. Connie and I have learned that even in mundane aspects of life, Holy Spirit teaches us to anticipate His leading. Every crisis, problem, or trial offers kingdom advancement with an opportunity to explore new possibilities. Faith works in times of trouble (see James 1:2-4).

I sometimes ask, "Who wants more faith"

Everyone raises his/her hand with a chorus of "Yes!" and "Amen!"

Then I pray, "Father, these saints desire more faith. Release trouble, trials, and tribulation into their lives so faith can be increased."

Shouts of "No!" quickly echo throughout the room! I then explain that faith operates during times when needed, for the gifts of healings and working of miracles come through situations that require it.

Jesus reminded disciples of the lesson concerning the miracle of the loaves and fishes. He walked on the sea during a storm; when He entered the disciples' boat, the wind ceased. Disciples were amazed and marveled at this miracle, "For they had not understood about the loaves, because their hearts were hardened" (Mark 6:52). How often have we forgotten or not understood the lesson the miracle should have taught us? Every miracle shows God's character, heart, and ways, which have power to conform us more to Christ's image. The kingdom principle of reproduction says every seed produces after its own kind (see Gen. 1:11). If we desire corn, we don't plant beans! Just so, miracles beget more miracles, particularly as we go into Holy Spirit's school of miracles to discover His deeper purposes and intents.

Conclusion

Miracles offer a tremendous platform for fully preaching the Gospel of Christ by demonstrating mighty signs and wonders through Holy

Spirit's power (see Rom. 15:19). Miracles are drawing cards attracting the unsaved as well as marginal believers into deeper relationship in Christ. Working of miracles provides a beautiful demonstration of Jesus' love like none other and should be considered *normal* Christianity. As with other gifts, working of miracles operates by faith. When you expect Holy Spirit to move in power and release covenant promises, He does! It's important not to question or be concerned about what others think—just do what you see Him doing and speak what you hear Him saying. I've long since stopped worrying about what people think about me. Many think we're fanatics, but to whom do you think they come when they need a miracle? Perhaps it's time to raise your vision to new levels of expectation to see God's miracle-working power manifested through you.

HARNESSING HIS POWER

Connie

When our parents took us Hunter kids to faith healers operating in God's power, we saw the lame throw down crutches, blind see, and terminally ill throw up cancers. Demons were cast out, and words of knowledge were answered by droves of people coming forward. We watched, enraptured by recurring miracles; when you see it so much, you believe it. That created a power heritage to know God's not only capable but He's also *going* to do it. Jesus said disciples would do even more than the amazing things He did because He sent "the Promise of My Father upon you; but tarry in the city of Jerusalem until you are endued with power from on high" (Luke 24:49). That power source for Oral Roberts, A.A. Allen, Katherine Kuhlman, William Branham, and many other mighty men and women of valor is that same Person who gives revelations and came upon disciples in that Jerusalem Upper Room—Holy Spirit.

Levels of Power

Holy Spirit's power is available to all born-again, Spirit-filled believers, but knowing that various levels exist is crucial. You learn about static electricity when someone walks across the carpet then touches your face. That little shock is significant, but it's not like getting a battery to power your flashlight to look in your crawl space. However, if you want to start your car, you certainly couldn't use the flashlight battery nor could that car battery power the light on your bedside table. Similarly, you couldn't connect your refrigerator into the same outlet your blow dryer uses. However, that potent kitchen outlet is just a fraction of the electrical power available from the power lines behind your house. They're all power, but they all vary in intensity. You need to learn to use them properly.

When you and I begin this power walk, we operate in various levels. At first, about all we can stand is static electricity, amazing but safe, as we progress in our walk. But eventually, static electricity can't accomplish what we need, so we go deeper into our power walk. That's a big leap, and sometimes God installs outlet protectors to keep us from getting into something we're too immature to touch. Some young Christians jump into the deep power place when they're ready for only the most basic. Impetuousness can devastate them and derail God's plans for them to grow into a mature Holy Spirit walk. God makes His power usable so its fullness is available as we progress. Just like we'd never let our young children play with or even plug something into a power source, so is this electric line power not for the spiritually immature. We can't touch the source or we'd die spiritually or be like Moses, whose face glowed from his transformer experience (see Exod. 34:29). God protects even our giftings.

God's Power

We understand God is mighty, yet sometimes we forget just how powerful He is. Moses described Him with "greatness and [a] mighty hand...[with incomparable] works and...mighty deeds" (Deut. 3:24). David said He's the "God who does wonders...[and] declare[s] His] strength among the peoples" (Ps. 77:14). Paul saw "the exceeding greatness of His power toward us who believe, according to the working of His mighty power" (Eph. 1:19). Job recognized God's might when he said "God thunders marvelously with His voice; He does great things which we cannot comprehend" (Job 37:5). Can we understand what these men are saying? Do we know God as the powerful entity He is? Even Christians have relegated Him to a corner to get blamed for the bad that happens but not regaled for His remarkable majesty and might beyond what our minds can fathom. Few understand the force of His character, El Shaddai, the Almighty One. He's freely shared that with us through Holy Spirit.

As I said in the "Words of Knowledge" chapter, we must remember that though amazing things happen as a result of our gifts, Holy Spirit is the source of the power, not us. Once, as Wade and I went to our car after a service, a lady was sitting in her car, waiting for her husband. She rolled down her window and started talking. Then she said she'd heard I could heal people.

"No," I told her. "I have a gift of miracles in my hands, but God heals."

"Oh, I know that," she said. She stared smiling at me for a moment. "It must be awesome to heal someone!"

"Well, that's an awesome gift for sure," I said, then shook my head. "But I don't heal. Holy Spirit does."

"Oh, I know that," she repeated, still staring with an awestruck expression. After a few seconds, she said, "Do you think you could heal my brother? He's in a lotta pain, and doctors can't help him."

I gave up. "Sure. Bring him by some time."

She smiled, and Wade and I went home. The next morning, before either of us was dressed, she called. "Connie?"

"Yeah."

"I told my brother you could heal him. He ran out and jumped in the car. We're on the way to your house now."

"Okay," I said. While I hurriedly dressed, they arrived. Wade and I met with her brother in our living room. He wasn't where he should be with God, so Wade talked about Jesus, and they prayed together. Then I took his hands, told him what to expect from Holy Spirit, and prayed. When I felt a release, he stood up and stretched, pain free. Wade asked him to do something he couldn't before. He touched his toes, eyes wide with wonder at God's miracle, which had proven Him mighty to that man.

No matter how we're acknowledged, we can stay humble despite our gifts' magnitude by remembering what we do is through Holy Spirit. The Lord gave Zerubbabel a battle cry we can remember as we go to war for things like healing. It's "'not by [our] might nor by [our] power, but by My Spirit,' says the Lord of hosts" (Zech. 4:6). God's using us, available vessels, to show His power and might. The Psalmist knew, "They did not gain possession of the land by their own sword, nor did their own arm save them; but it was Your right hand, Your arm, and the light of Your countenance" (Ps. 44:3). It's all Him!

I love how disciples kept this in perspective. In Acts 3, they'd been instrumental in healing the lame man at the Gate Beautiful. In chapter 4, the miracle was so highly publicized that five thousand were saved. Despite the hoopla, Peter stayed humble. As others raved about the healing, "When Peter saw it, he responded to the people: 'Men of Israel, why do you marvel at this? Or why look so intently at us, as though by our own power or godliness we had made this man walk?'" (Acts 3:12). He's saying, "It's not me. I can't do anything without God." Amen!

Once, the Lord told me I was like an extension cord between His extreme power and the need. Peter understood he was just the conduit too, the extension cord that connected to that Source who brought the crippled man's healing into reality. If we arrive at this power walk and give praise "to God our Savior, who alone is wise" (Jude 25), we'll keep both crucial aspects of our gifts—humility and love—in perspective. Many great generals whom God has used mightily have fallen because they allowed pride to creep in and neglected to give God the glory He was due. It's not about us!

Heritage of Power

Stepping into this walk begins by understanding Holy Spirit's power within us. When we're saved, through Jesus' name we have exousia, "ability; privilege...force, capacity...authority, jurisdiction...power, right, strength."[1] Exousia means authority because we call on Jesus' name with unlimited power for everything from salvation to miracles. Just as the potter has exousia to make the clay (see Rom. 9:21), it's in our hands through Holy Spirit to appropriate that creative ability for meeting needs. Our legal authority comes through Jesus' sacrifice.

The other type of power is dunamis. The word itself means "power," as do its derivatives—*dunamai* ("to be able"),[2] *dunamoo* ("strengthen"),[3] *dunateo* ("be mighty"),[4] *dunatos* ("powerful or capable").[5] From combinations of Greek words come powerful English words too—*dynamite, dynasty, dynamic.* Dunamis is "force...miraculous power...ability, abundance...might, (worker of) miracle(s)...strength, violence, mighty (wonderful) work."[6] I love the one about violence—power so strong it holds a violent connotation. Holy Spirit's character has abundant, violent power. Can we get each of these into our spirits and know this power is beyond imagination?

Stephen (see Acts 6:8), Jesus (see Acts 10:38), Paul (see Rom. 15:19), even God (see Luke 22:69) operated with dunamis power. Holy Spirit's power has come and given full access to dunamis and all that comes with it. Oh and by the way, though satan is described as also having dunamis, if all we had were exousia, we could defeat him because just mentioning Jesus' name sends the enemy running (see Luke 10:19). Add to that Holy Spirit's dunamis, and he can't prevail. He's defeated by unbeatable power and authority.

Virtue

So God has created this power and wants us to use it to exalt Him (see Exod. 9:16). However, we should begin at the static-electricity phase and graduate to higher levels as we mature. This is the process that has brought me into increased levels of Holy Spirit's power. This transformer power is extreme and evolved over the course of years. Long ago, I dreamed I stopped people in cars and asked if they needed a miracle because God told me, "There's healing in your hands." In reality, after that I saw more of that gift operate. When I'd lay hands on people as I ministered, they'd feel intense heat or electricity. At a service in Tennessee, I ministered to a woman who was already slain in the Spirit. As I grabbed her ankles, she jumped like she'd been touched by the paddles of life. Other times, people have said my hands were so hot that they could hardly hold them. Then my pastor had a dream that I was praying for people and fire shot from my hands. That seemed to be when God catapulted me into something deeper. Each time I'd hear these descriptions and feel God activating this new power level, I saw potency I'd never experienced.

I wasn't sure how to label this gift, so I described it as infusing something from me into someone else. As I read Jesus' account of how His power worked, though, I realized He'd already named it. In Mark 5, a woman with a flow of blood for twelve years knew if she could touch His garment, she'd be healed. She did. "And Jesus, immediately knowing in Himself that power [dunamis (*virtue* in KJV)] had gone out of Him, turned around in the crowd and said, 'Who touched My clothes?'" (Mark 5:30). When Luke tells the story, Jesus says, "Somebody touched Me, for I perceived power going out from Me" (Luke 8:46). Another time, a multitude sought to touch Him. That description says "power went out from Him and [He] healed them all" (Luke 6:19).

These descriptions perfectly summarize the sensation as this power gift operates. I don't infuse into others unless I feel led to; but when I do, something happens. As I take their hands and wait on the Spirit, He often leads me to pray in tongues or at times just to continue waiting on Him. God gives a direction to pray, or I speak for Holy Spirit to "aim the power at the need." Then, my right hand vibrates or I go into travail and know an amazing breakthrough is happening. When it's complete, I literally feel virtue leave my body. As it goes, that power does the intended work. People feel varied sensations—tingling, hot hands, jolts, electricity, vibrations. The power's so intense that it's usually difficult to stand, so both of us are often slain in the Spirit as power leaves my body and enters theirs.

One night at a service, people all around the room were ministering in groups as God led. Someone asked me to pray for four women at different stages of sorrow. As I approached, the Lord told me they should join hands; as I completed that circuit, electricity would travel around the circle. As I took my spot and grabbed two ladies' hands, power hit me so strongly I dropped their hands and collapsed. I wasn't the only one. I don't know how long I was slain in the Spirit; but when I could open my eyes, all five of us were lying in a round formation on the tile. Holy Spirit had done such a work with His electric circle that not only were they touched, but I was too. I was so weak, though, Wade had to help me to the car. With this gift, the more people I infuse, the weaker I get because power literally leaves my body each time. I guess that may be one reason Jesus had to find time to replenish His energy. One night, I infused into about thirty people and could barely get out of bed the next day. What a great problem!

Conclusion

When the woman touched Jesus' garment (see Matt. 9:20) or when Jesus touched blind eyes (see Matt. 20:34), deaf tongues (see Mark 7:33), leprous bodies (see Matt. 8:3), or a friend's mother-in-law (see Matt. 8:15), each touch healed them by that dunamis power that resided in the Master. However, as virtue, that power, left Him and went into others' bodies to touch their desperate needs, He did something else. That touch, *haptomai*, means "to attach oneself to."[7] Imagine that! The Lord's touch bonds Him to us and us to Him inextricably. As our hand touches another to minister healing or deliverance, it's Jesus' hand through ours, attaching itself to the need. With faith as the glue, His touch becomes affixed as it haptomais itself to us and changes the unchangeable or heals the unhealable. His touch is just the right power level to accomplish anything.

When I first began to operate in this power gift, I was in awe. I'd never seen this intensity up close, operating in this way or magnitude; but though years have now passed, I'm still humbled each time someone is touched by the Lord's hand through mine. I don't always know what that virtue will accomplish. Sometimes people come for physical healing and go away with a different type of healing inside. Healing may be physical, emotional, spiritual, or any combination of things, but power comes to meet those needs.

Do you want to move toward a more powerful walk than the static electricity you've grown accustomed to? Through intimacy, we draw nearer to Him and He gets nearer to us. How? Through worship. Praise brings worship, which brings glory, which brings power. John describes this glory scene: "The temple was filled with smoke from the glory of God and from His power, and no one was able to enter the temple" (Rev. 15:8). When something needs to be replenished in me so I have power to give others, I spend time in that glory. It makes me ready to give out as needs come. It's wondrous, exciting, and effective. It's our high-voltage Holy Spirit power.

ONE TO GROW ON: INTERCESSION

Wade

Military campaigns are typically initiated with intensive aerial attacks. Remember the "shock and awe" bombardments of the Iraqi campaign? In like manner, intercession is spiritual air war utilizing speaking gifts and prophetic action to release Holy Spirit's shock and awe on enemy strongholds. Intercession is the spiritual concept of natural air war. This spiritual air attack releases angelic hosts on the enemy, creating havoc and chaos in his ranks. Natural air power is concentrated on strategic targets, making the enemy vulnerable and open to exploitation. The same is true for spiritual intercession. Holy Spirit directs prophetic actions, rendering satan's spiritual hierarchy ineffective and defenseless (see Eph. 6:12). Holy Spirit's acts of power displace and destroy the enemy's bondage on lives.

Intercession is where the Spirit's weapons are employed. Most think intercession is a prayer meeting where some of the church women gather during the week to go over prayer requests. In most fellowships, this prayer time is the least attended yet one of the most important! Intercession is the ministry of a priest (intercessor) standing in the gap between the messes of life and spiritual reality of God's truth. They use Father's language—calling those things which are not as though they were (see Rom. 4:17), so words become earthly reality. Intercession is literally living on behalf of others, using weapons of warfare to destroy the devil's works (see 1 John 3:8).

Intercession

God has been seeking intercessors since man's fall. Speaking through prophets, the Lord declared His need for an intercessor:

> *He saw that there was no man, and wondered that there was no intercessor; therefore His own arm brought salvation for Him; and His own righteousness, it sustained Him* (Isaiah 59:16).

> *I looked, but there was no one to help, and I wondered that there was no one to uphold; therefore My own arm brought salvation for Me; and My own fury, it sustained Me* (Isaiah 63:5).

The Old Covenant Hebrew word for *intercession* is *paga*, "to impinge, by accident or violence, or by importunity—come (betwixt), cause to entreat, fall (upon), make intercession, intercessor, entreat, lay, light (upon), meet (together), pray, reach, run."[1] These meanings obviously imply both speaking and acting. In our ministry experience, we've seen intercession take the following forms.

Spiritual Warfare

Intercession is ministry where satan's kingdom is destroyed and displaced with God's Kingdom reality. Old Covenant battles correlate to New Covenant spiritual warfare, most of which occurs between our ears. Second Corinthians 10:3-6 explains that spiritual warfare pulls down strongholds—areas of darkness (ignorance) in our minds that aren't exposed to Holy Spirit's illumination of truth. The mind is the battleground where the enemy must be uprooted and cast out; otherwise, he'll continue to negatively influence one's thought life. Proverbs 23:7 states, "For as he thinks in his heart, so is he." Just as the Israelites were instructed by God to utterly destroy the seven nations occupying the Promised Land (see Deut. 7:1-2), we're to utterly destroy strongholds in our promised land—life in Christ.

The outcome of spiritual warfare should never be in doubt. Satan was defeated at the cross and through Jesus' resurrection. Our position in spiritual warfare is to enforce the victory already ours in

Christ. Too many have a victim's mentality when in Christ they've been made more than conquerors (see Rom. 8:37). Fear-based prayers cause the belief that we're powerless against the enemy's attack. This is a result of ignorance of God's Word and covenant promises. Unfortunately, many prayer meetings begin with fear-filled prayer requests and end with, "Well, I hope God heard." God responds to faith, not fear. When words are fear-based, we're reinforcing the enemy's stronghold, calling it prayer. Spiritual warfare is an act of victorious celebration in the face of apparent defeat. Intercession doesn't ignore facts of life; it violently engages those temporary facts with eternal truth of God's Word, knowing His truth will supersede, override, and cancel those facts through faith.

Burden Bearing

Intercession also includes sharing another's load. Paul encouraged believers to "Bear one another's burdens, and so fulfill the law of Christ" (Gal. 6:2). The law of Christ is to bear, or *bastazo*, others' burdens. This word bastazo carries the meaning of removal, so we're not to lug around someone else's load of problems, leading to burn-out. Through Holy Spirit's power, in intercession, we're to remove satan's burdens from others. The prophet Isaiah explained: "It shall come to pass in that day that his burden will be taken away from your shoulder, and his yoke from your neck, and the yoke will be destroyed because of the anointing oil" (Isa. 10:27). Jesus Christ (the Anointed One) is our example of the perfect Intercessor. He says:

> *Come to Me, all you who labor and are heavy laden, and I will give you rest. Take My yoke upon you and learn from Me, for I am gentle and lowly in heart, and you will find rest for your souls. For My yoke is easy and My burden is light* (Matthew 11:28-30).

The question is, whose load are we bearing—God's or satan's? Our intercession is to remove and dispose of fear, sickness, disease, poverty, bitterness, and all effects of the curse the enemy authors to steal, kill, and destroy (see John 10:10).

189

Putting Satan under Our Feet

From the day of man's expulsion from the garden, satan (the serpent) was cursed by God to assume the spiritual position of crawling on his belly and eating earth's dust (see Gen. 3:14). For mankind, this can be good or bad news, depending on where you're spiritually positioned. The bad news—man was created from dust (see Gen. 2:7), so unconverted man is nothing more than devil's food. The good news—for believers, satan is under our feet! Jesus gave His disciples authority to trample on the enemy and not be hurt by anything he throws at them (see Luke 10:19). Paul wrote, "And the God of peace will crush Satan under your feet shortly" (Rom. 16:20). Our intercession is to tread on the enemy and his schemes.

An Old Covenant example of this is in Joshua 10, where Israel battled against five kings of the Amorites, meaning "bitter; a rebel."[2] In this battle, God cast down large hailstones, killing many; at Joshua's command, the sun stood still, causing Israel to prevail. The kings' names were Adoni-Zedek ("lord of justice"),[3] Hoham ("woe to them"),[4] Piram ("a wild ass of them"),[5] Japhia ("enlightening"),[6] and Debir ("an orator").[7] These names' meanings directly apply to lucifer's character and desire to usurp God's position (see Isa. 14:12-17). When the kings hid in a cave, Joshua ordered the cave opened and the kings brought out. He commanded his captains to put their feet on the kings' necks, symbolic of our authority over the enemy's power (see Josh. 10:24-25).

Divine Protection

Intercessors are under Almighty God's protective cover. First John 5:18 gives assurance that we're positioned where the evil one doesn't touch us. The psalmist describes God's divine protection as the "secret place…[a] refuge and fortress…[and a place of safety with] His truth [as our] shield and buckler" (Ps. 91:1,2,4). God's covenant promises are realized by faith with willingness and obedience to the Spirit's prompting. Intercession is a place of boldness in the face of impossibilities. As intercessors, we can be assured of God's divine protection and authority to extend His victory over sin and its consequences.

Paul describes God's divine protection as the full armor of God. Ephesians 6:10-17 uses a soldier's armor as a metaphor to describe our battle garb for spiritual warfare, activated by "praying always with all prayer and supplication in the Spirit" (Eph. 6:18). Being fully furnished with God's armor symbolizes believers being in Christ, standing victorious over the enemy's schemes. With His full armor, we're girded with the belt of truth, fitted with the breastplate of righteousness, shod with the Gospel of peace, given the shield of faith to extinguish the enemy's fiery darts, and receive the helmet of salvation. Protected with His full armor, we have boldness to live in victory defended by God's very character.

His armor is our defense, but He also provides our offensive weapon—the sword of the Spirit (see Eph. 6:17). This sword is not the long battle sword but the short sword of sacrifice, meaning it represents rhema—Holy Spirit's proceeding word (see Matt. 4:4). The rhema word is our weapon to destroy the enemy's works. It's through our praying in the Spirit (tongues) that we engage the sword of the Spirit. Tongues are Holy Spirit's words that powerfully act to destroy the enemy's tactics. The "full armor of God" is a symbolic picture of our position "in Christ" and Holy Spirit's anointing. Properly armored believers look exactly like Lord Jesus Christ to our enemy. In God's armor, we stand victorious over his devices, just as Jesus conquered death, hell, and the grave.

Travail as in Childbirth

Intercession often requires spiritual travail to transfer God's promises from the Spirit realm to the natural. Just as a woman in childbirth, travail is our interceding to bring forth God's promise. Tremendous deliverance and healings result from travail. In some cases, travail is a private ministry; at other times, Holy Spirit brings travail when praying in public. This often happens with Connie as she prays and stands in the gap between the problem and God's solution. It's not pretty nor dignified (Connie admits her travail sounds like a bull moose in distress), but boy is it powerful!

One of the most effective travail warriors I've known was Shawn, our worship leader when we pastored. Whenever someone came forward with an impossibility requiring a miracle, I'd ask Shawn to minister to him/her. He didn't need to be aware of the situation because Holy Spirit knew the solution and used Shawn to break through frozen circumstances. Once, Connie saw a vision of him as a jackhammer shattering hard concrete because his intercessory travail regularly broke through into Holy Spirit's miracle realm. As travail came over him, he wept and groaned in agony, even going to the floor in a curled-up position. Shawn, unpretentious, quiet, and gentle, operated in travail that was loud and full of grief and agony. After a time, he would remain quietly on the floor, seemingly asleep. After a few moments, I'd hear soft chuckles that gave way to all-out laughter and contagious deep-belly guffaws. At that point, I knew breakthrough was accomplished and the miracle was on its way. What an awesome gift!

Paul wrote, "My little children, for whom I labor in birth again until Christ be formed in you" (Gal. 4:19). Obviously, Paul understood travail and its powerful intercessory effect. Recently, Derek, an associate pastor where we attend church, entered travail for the first time. Unable to stand, he went to the floor with several men around him wondering what was happening. I told them to leave him alone—the Spirit was doing a work of intercession through him. After Derek had broken through by travailing, I asked how he felt. He had no idea what had happened to him, but he knew Holy Spirit was up to something special. I explained that he'd just experienced Holy Spirit's breakthrough travail, a new dimension of deliverance ministry. Since that time, he's had other travail experiences and is *on fire* for God. That's travail's power!

Divine Intersections

Intercession isn't always a planned event. Intercessory services are awesome, but the most powerful times occur when we "light upon" situations requiring immediate action. Jesus demonstrated this intercession aspect. Once, as He was teaching a woman came with a spirit of infirmity, causing her to be bent over and unable to raise herself for eighteen years. Jesus said, "Woman, you are loosed from your infirmity" (Luke 13:12) and laid hands on her. She immediately stood up straight and glorified God. Life is filled with divine intersections when intercession and Holy Spirit's power are required to displace a cursed situation with the reality of God's Kingdom. These are opportunities to turn life's messes into God's miracles!

Lightning Anointing

In this form of intercession, prophetic actions release a lightning anointing causing the enemy to "cease and desist" his activity and reverse his actions. Here, compassion rises, and Holy Spirit's power is released through intercessors. Resurrection power flows from this lightning anointing. Job describes this best: "He covers His hands with lightning, and commands it to strike" (Job 36:32). We've often seen this lightning anointing leave miracles in its wake. With this anointing, heat is released and often felt in those ministered to. Heat's release occurs when forms of energy change. This is called entropy, an aspect of the second law of thermodynamics. When resurrection dunamis power is released within bodies, it changes form and becomes usable to heal affected areas. That's why people often feel heat while being healed. Under lightning anointing, a simple hand waving or blowing in a certain direction will have the magnified effect, causing people to be slain in the Spirit, healed, or delivered. This anointing is accompanied and magnified by angelic ministry, causing healings and miracles to become commonplace.

Gift of Suffering

As Connie mentioned before, the gift of suffering is an amazing weapon. This aspect of intercession isn't for the uninitiated in spiritual warfare. Paul describes the gift of suffering in three Scriptures—Romans 8:16-17, Philippians 1:29, and Colossians 1:24. He emphasized that suffering in Christ is a means through which His glory manifests. This gift of suffering has nothing to do with permitting satan's schemes of bringing sickness, disease, poverty, lack, confusion, fear, depression, or anything related to the curse from which we've been redeemed. Of course, different degrees of suffering exist.

Jesus Christ came to be our heavenly Representative; we're to be His representatives right here, right now (see John 17:18). Jesus demonstrated life as a divine Transfer Agent of heaven's reality to earth, so we're to be transfer agents of Holy Spirit's abilities as dual-realm creations (see 2 Cor. 5:17). Just as Jesus took sin to the cross, so also we're to bear others' burdens (see Gal. 6:2). Although Jesus became the curse for us, the curse and its effects still exist. Bearing others' burdens becomes our responsibility as intercessors. So how does the gift of suffering operate?

I was introduced to this gift by my former Pastor Ruth Hoskins. Ironically, she'd begun operating in this gift after Connie's father, her pastor, had laid hands on her years before when she asked to go deeper into intercessory ministry. This was activated in me, too, by her laying on hands. Almost immediately, unusual physical manifestations occurred. One night, I suffered pains in my side and lower back similar to kidney stones. When I prayed in the Spirit, pain subsided then completely stopped; when I stopped praying in the Spirit, pain came back full force. That's how I knew this was the gift of suffering with a divine intercessory assignment. For me, praying in the Spirit, along with prophetic declarations for the pain's cause to cease and desist, was how this ministry was to be conducted. Connie's gift operates differently. When she gets a distinct feeling, she knows timing or proximity is right for it to be for another.

My first few exposures with the gift of suffering took several hours to minister through to complete deliverance and healing. As I grew in this gift, I learned to break through in minutes. Since then, both Connie and I have interceded for many others' physical and mental conditions. As I've taught on this gift, several people have thanked me because they had similar experiences but didn't know how to pray through. They explained that now, instead of fear, they operate in faith as they embrace these divine intercessory assignments. What a marvelous gift and honor to be used by God in intercession in such a way!

Other aspects of effective paga include (1) *kairos*, "an occasion, i.e. set or proper time,"[8] (2) *episkiazo*, "to cast a shade upon...to envelop in a haze of brilliancy...overshadow,"[9] and (3) *metanoia*, "compunction (for guilt)...reversal (of [another's] decision), repentance."[10] It's divine partnership with Christ in His present-day ministry as our Great High Priest. The New Covenant Greek word for *intercession* is *entugchano*, which means "to chance upon...confer with...to entreat (in favor of or against); deal with; make intercession."[11] It carries all meanings of paga and more. This word for intercession is used in Paul's letter to the church at Rome:

> *Likewise the Spirit also helps in our weaknesses. For we do not know what we should pray as we ought, but the Spirit Himself makes intercession for us with groanings which cannot be uttered. Now He who searches the hearts knows what the mind of the Spirit is, because He makes intercession for the saints according to the will of God* (Romans 8:26-27).

Intercession is authored and initiated by Holy Spirit, and He alone knows how to pray for situations. From our carnal minds, we're praying with our opinions, not from a divine perspective. We have a major weakness because we don't know how to pray effectively and may even hinder God's will. I would rather have intercessors praying for me in the Spirit than from their own opinions. Holy Spirit knows beginning from end and all in between!

Principle of Dominion

Intercession demonstrates the Kingdom principle of dominion (governorship) (see Gen.1:26). God gave man dominion on earth. Dominion is best demonstrated in partnership with Holy Spirit. When we pray in the Spirit with utterances we can't understand, He's praying through us as we give Him our physical capabilities.

In 1971, I was serving as a military advisor to Vietnamese troops in protecting districts from NVA and Vietcong infiltration. These ill-trained troops had a habit of running away at the first gunfire. On this particular day, I was with the lead squad of a patrol, searching out a supposedly evacuated NVA defensive position. We were ambushed at close range. A B40 rocket used by the NVA for antitank warfare was fired directly at me; the explosion's shock knocked me to the ground. When I regained my composure, I realized I hadn't been hit—miraculously. The tree directly behind where I was walking was completely sawn off from the waist up!

Upon returning home, my mother asked what had happened on that day because Holy Spirit had impressed on her to intercede in the Spirit for several hours. That was the source of my miracle protection and why I walked away unscathed. At that time, I was a practicing sinner, yet Holy Spirit interceded through Mom and spared my life. That's intercession's power!

We're His "royal priesthood" (1 Pet. 2:9). Kings demonstrate dominion or governorship; priests are intercessors. We're both. As intercessors, we determine which environment exists on earth—heaven or hell. In this role as God's "royal priesthood," through Holy Spirit's guidance, we're in partnership with the Lord Jesus Christ in His present-day ministry as our Great High Priest. Hebrews 7:24-25 says:

> But He, because He continues forever, has an unchangeable priesthood. Therefore He is also able to save to the uttermost those who come to God through Him, since He always lives to make intercession for them.

Conclusion

Intercession is the ministry of the hour where heaven's resources are available to believers in our role as kings and priests. The present-day ministry of Jesus Christ at the Father's right hand is to make intercession for saints through Holy Spirit within us. Romans 8:28 says,

"And we know that all things work together for good to those who love God, to those who are called according to His purpose." What's His purpose? Intercession. Here's the reality—Jesus Christ is in partnership with believers who are intercessors through the Spirit. As we intercede through prophetic actions and declarations, Jesus intercedes with us through His Spirit. Paul explained in his letter to the church at Corinth that believers are "workers together with Him," or co-laborers with Christ (2 Cor. 6:1). This truth of partnership is never more fully realized than in intercession!

AFTERWORD

Wade

This book has been a labor of love for Connie and me. As we've reminisced about how Holy Spirit has blessed us and others through His gifts, we've fallen even deeper in love with Him. I'm reminded of Romans 5:5: "Now hope does not disappoint, because the love of God has been poured out in our hearts by the Holy Spirit who was given us." Perhaps this is the greatest ministry of all—pouring out God's love into our hearts. By pouring it out, faith is increased because faith works by love (see Gal. 5:6). Our desire is for everyone to love Him as we do and be open for Him to reveal more of Himself.

Although we've experienced His gifts firsthand and helped others discover Him as well, we've just begun our Holy Spirit journey. The *finished work* of Jesus is a progressive revelation of Holy Spirit's wisdom, knowledge, and understanding. This progression is from "glory to glory, just as by the Spirit of the Lord" (2 Cor. 3:18). In Holy Spirit, we not only experience God's love but also become His hand extended to others. That's my simple explanation of Paul's meaning in his letters when he often wrote, "in Christ" (Eph. 1:3, for example). It's more than a position; it's a calling, a commission, a mandate. It's becoming a container-expresser of God's love.

Having filled various ministry roles—pastors, teachers, evangelists, writers—Connie and I knew Holy Spirit had other work for us; we just didn't know details. Long ago, He impressed me that our ministry was to equip equippers. As pastors, we did what we could to move people to a higher spiritual level, but most of the time was spent dealing with spiritual babies and teens—and that's what pastors do. Holy Spirit has orchestrated a new role—to train others by honing and sharpening spiritual weapons of warfare and tools of harvest. In short, we're equipping saints for the work of Holy Spirit's ministry.

Ministry Commission

In 2009, Holy Spirit commissioned us to provide a platform for *activation, elevation,* and *acceleration.* He inspired us to start a home Bible study, which grew into our Times of Refreshing services where He moves in signs and wonders. Soon after starting our Bible study, Holy Spirit inspired Connie to write *God's Plan for Our Success, Nehemiah's Way* and provided a publisher, Destiny Image, to release her book. We were also directed to organize and conduct all-day workshops that instructed others about how to use their gifts and advance toward their destinies. Holy Spirit has continued to affirm this mandate and open doors for our ministry. We also believe this book occupies an important part of that mandate to provide activation, elevation, and acceleration.

Activation: Baptism of Holy Spirit

After His death, burial, and resurrection, Jesus appeared to His disciples and said,

> *"Peace to you! As the Father has sent Me, I also send you." And when He had said this, He breathed on them, and said to them, "Receive the Holy Spirit. If you forgive the sins of any, they are forgiven them; if you retain the sins of any, they are retained"* (John 20:21-23).

Later, Jesus commanded His disciples to wait for the Father's promise—baptism of Holy Spirit (see Acts 1:4-5). Jesus said, "But you shall receive power when the Holy Spirit has come upon you; and you shall be witnesses to Me in Jerusalem, and in all Judea and Samaria, and to the end of the earth" (Acts 1:8). If those closest to Jesus were to wait and receive the baptism of Holy Spirit before they ministered, how much more do we need Holy Spirit? Are we so educated, polished, and sophisticated that we don't need His divine enablement? Without Holy Spirit and His gifts operating, how will we ever participate in the same and greater works (see John 14:12) Jesus promised? Perhaps some will join me in making Jesus' words their motto, just as it is mine: "If I don't do the works of My Father, then don't believe Me" (John 10:37). Some first century believers turned the world upside down (see Acts 17:6). Jesus hasn't changed; He's the same yesterday, today, and forever. Let's join Him in turning the world right side up by seeing Holy Spirit activated in believers' lives.

Elevation: Change of Perspective: Going to New Levels
Too many believe only what they perceive with natural sight. Once Holy Spirit has been activated in a believer's life, elevation is required for true "vision" to occur. Proverbs 29:18 (KJV) states, "Where there is no vision, the people perish." Vision, a prophetic revelation, is not only inspired but also apprehended by Holy Spirit. Revelation 4:1 is a command issued to change perspective—"Come up here, and I will show you things which must take place after this." From being seated in heavenly places, a believer receives spiritual vision to view beyond the temporary, illusionary realm of the seen into the invisible, eternal realm of the Spirit (see 2 Cor. 4:18). Elevation speaks of renewing the mind, essential for operating in God's will (see Rom. 12:1-2). Once perceived through prophetic revelation (vision), all things become possible. If you can "see" it, you can have it!

Acceleration: Suddenly
Once a believer is properly positioned in Christ, acceleration is the natural consequence. The speed of light is 186,000 miles per second; the speed of glory is *now!* To be in Christ is to be in the glory zone of God's presence. Once God speaks through His logos or Holy Spirit's rhema, reality of His word is created in the spiritual realm. Faith is the vehicle that transfers manifestation from the spirit realm to the

natural. Hebrews 11:3 explains, "By faith we understand that the worlds were framed by the word of God, so that the things which are seen were not made of things which are visible." Within the glory zone of God's presence—in Christ—we intercede and minister Kingdom reality into earth's environment as transfer agents (see 2 Cor. 1:20). Results of obedience are instantaneous Kingdom manifestations. God accelerates His purpose through willingness and obedience. Isaiah 60:22 declares that, "I, the Lord, will hasten it in its time." As believers grow in understanding God's glory (see Hab. 2:14), Holy Spirit hastens manifestations. Once in prayer, Holy Spirit impressed on me that I would live to participate in a worldwide move of God which would become known as "Pray and Duck." Holy Spirit's instantaneous answers to prayer and prophetic declarations would come so rapidly that once spoken, you'd better duck because the answer's on the way. That's acceleration!

Holy Spirit Highway

Many in the church stand at a crossroad. You can continue on the well-marked highway, heavily traveled and predictable with familiar fast-food restaurants having the usual fare. This is the way you're used to, the way you've always gone; it presents no danger of getting lost. The other route is one you've not traveled. You've heard it has dangerous turns, is unpredictable, looks frightening, and isn't safe. But a stirring in your spirit says this is the way you should go. This way is full of new adventure, and you'll discover new meaning and purpose. You'd heard rumors the restaurants on this road serve all types of food; you can order from a menu of all God has to offer, not just what's fried, quick, and on a bun. Could it be that this new road will get you to your destination quicker than the old, familiar road that seems to wind on continually?

Let me encourage you to take the new road. I've been on both. The first is church as usual—religious ritual, devoid of Holy Spirit's presence and power. The second road is filled with excitement, joy, and wonder in discovery of your new life in Christ. This is the road of which the prophet Isaiah wrote:

> *Prepare the way of the Lord; make straight in the desert a highway for our God. Every valley shall be exalted and every mountain and hill brought low; the crooked places shall be made straight and the rough places smooth; the glory of the Lord shall be revealed, and all flesh shall see it together; for the mouth of the Lord has spoken* (Isaiah 40:3-5).

Tell me, how could you possibly want to go any other way?

Connie

We live in a world full of hazards in everything from food additives to air pollution. We follow doctors' directions only to find out years later that his course of action caused horrific effects. We can fall prey to carjacking, home invaders, identity theft, and even unscrupulous friends with their own agendas. With all this around us, how do we ever rest or trust or believe? We give it to Holy Spirit and know He's our consummate Teacher, Illuminator, Protector, Counselor, Guide, Encourager, Helper, and Comforter. He warns of danger and then gives tools and weapons to make it through. He's our key to power. By giving Him our needs and allowing Him to use us in His way and time, we're overcomers.

As Wade and I compiled what God put on our hearts for this book, we thought about experiences we should include so your Holy Spirit walk could be richer and more powerful. The numerous happenings we've shared are just a fraction of what we see Him do daily. Many other people have much more knowledge than we do, so wonderful mentors exist who can bring you along in your gifts. As I said in my preface, everyone is at various levels of operating in Holy Spirit; so if you're using your gifts and desire to grow deeper, wherever you are in your progression of moving in the Spirit, you're okay. You don't have to be perfect, just teachable. As you mature, each experience leads to God's plan for you, and the knowledge you glean about the gifts makes you a conqueror. Here's a summary of the Spirit's gifts and examples from ours, our families', and our friends' lives that brought overcoming power to defeat the enemy.

Revelation

Words of Knowledge
God speaks to you that the person at the next table in the restaurant is having problems with his hand. That's a word of knowledge. Amazed, he confirms it's been hurting many years. You pray; he's able to move his fingers better than he has in a long time, and he sees God cares for him. That's power.

Words of Knowledge—Unction

One night when you're preaching at a service, God speaks into your spirit that someone has a growth that will melt like butter. That's a word of knowledge, an unction. A lady with a lump on her neck comes forward. Before the service's end, that growth has diminished so much it's nearly gone. That's power.

Words of Knowledge—Vision

One day, when you're speaking at a retreat, God shows you a lady's ear. That's a word of knowledge, a vision. While you pray, you call out for her ear to be healed. Later, she testifies that she had ear damage that impeded her ability to hear background noise. After prayer, she can hear everything, even the soft music played during ministry. That's power.

Words of Wisdom—Unction

Your friend's daughter has dinner with her friends. They all start home. As she drives, the daughter feels like she shouldn't follow them on her usual route but rather goes a longer way. That's a word of wisdom, an unction. The next morning, she's awakened by the police who say her friends had been in an accident on the road that she'd nearly taken. The wife had been killed. Your friend's daughter would have certainly perished had she been driving in the car behind them. That's power.

Words of Wisdom—Vision

When you're praying, God shows you a man in the congregation who's hurt down inside a concrete pit. That's a word of wisdom in a vision. When you tell him, his wife says he'll be working in a cistern the next day. He works and nothing happens. That's power.

Words of Wisdom—Dream

A sister dreams that another sister, a prison guard, is held with a knife to her throat. That's a word of wisdom through a dream. Your family prays fervently. A short time later, the sister about whom she'd dreamed and another guard are taken captive by prisoners who hold knives to their throats. The hostage situation is resolved with no injuries. That's power.

Discernment of Spirits

You know something's wrong with the man for whom you're working. That's discernment of spirits. You resign and cut off ties with him. About a year later, you hear he's bilked many people and is going to prison. Several employees have guilt by association, but you don't. That's power.

Speaking

Tongues, Interpretation, Prophecy

One night, your teenaged sister feels led to put her hands on the front of a young man's neck, speak a message in tongues, then give an interpretation. That's tongues and interpretation, which lead to prophecy. As she prophesies, she speaks God's word—He's always with him and will protect and guide him. Within two weeks, the young man is attacked in an alley and his throat is slit. Though doctors pronounce sentences to the contrary, he not only survives but also ultimately has his speech fully restored. That's power.

Tongues—Prayer Language

You don't perceive what's wrong, but you know you must pray immediately. As you allow Holy Spirit to intercede for you, you realize you must get your children into the house. That's a word of wisdom brought through prayer language. You call them from where they're sledding on the hill near your home. As they're going in the kitchen door, a loud noise makes everyone stop. From the weight of the ice, electric lines had fallen onto the location where your children were playing. Had Holy Spirit not quickened into your spirit that they should come home, they all would have certainly died. That's power.

Prophecy

A word comes to you in the fall that when time springs forward, you'll get a contract for the book you've written. That's prophecy.

Despite what happens and how circumstances look to the contrary in the ensuing months, you stand on that word. Your contract comes in the spring shortly after the time changes. That's power.

Power

Faith

God speaks to you and says you should ignore a negative report your daughter will receive at her doctor's appointment the next week. That's the gift of faith brought about by a word of wisdom. On Monday, she calls crying hysterically because of the report. You refuse to believe anything but God's word could be true. The doctor calls that same day to say he made a mistake and she's fine. That's power.

Gifts of Healings

You're staying in a dorm room at a camp meeting when your diabetic friend sees an angel come in and touch her. That's a gift of healing brought by a supernatural being. The next and subsequent days, her insulin makes her sick like she's taken too much. She reduces her dosage until finally she takes none. When she returns to the doctor, he tells her to continue taking that amount because her glucose level is perfect. That's power.

Word of Knowledge—Gift of Suffering—Miracle

One day as you're teaching at a Holy Spirit workshop, you feel pain in your back. No one responds when you give the word, so you continue teaching. When the pain worsens, you stop again and say you know someone has problems with his/her back, point to the area, and describe the pain. That's a word of knowledge through a gift of suffering that leads to a miracle. A woman responds, receives prayer, and feels the pain leave. A few months later, she testifies that she had at first hesitated about responding because she was skeptical about the gifts. However, she had gone to the doctor that week. Her back pain had been caused by spinal taps for a tumor behind her eye. The doctor pronounces the eye healed. That's power.

Word of Knowledge—Prophetic Action—Miracle

One night at a Bible study, God tells you to put your finger on some-one's infected toe, and your finger will be God's finger to dry up that infection. That's a word of knowledge leading to the working of miracles through a prophetic action. The woman who responds cringes as your finger nears her toe because it's so sore even the bed sheet hurts. Not only does God's finger through yours not hurt her that night; but by evening's end, pain is gone and infection is dried up. That's power.

Conclusion

Like the story I related in my preface about Jill and language, many times, my daughters' growth has paralleled my learning from my Father. The day they were eligible for their learners' permits, we headed out bright and early to the license branch. They had plans that we'd go to the movies in Richmond, Indiana, about thirty miles away, and they'd get to practice their driving craft on the way there and back. The arrangement sounded good, but they'd overlooked one detail—Wade was away on business and had driven our only car with an automatic transmission. They would need to drive our little car with a stick shift.

The trip to the movies and back was scary. The motor's revving and bouncy starts were difficult, just like for all of us who learned to shift. The problem was that just plain driving was a skill they should have been learning that day. They needed to watch for stop signs, pedestrians, darting deer, speed limits, and other vehicles. They needed to see how to pass and ease the car back into their lane while looking at everything else in the road around them. They needed to apply what the training manual had taught but now had practi-cal meaning as they traversed those country roads. They needed to master basics before they focused on easing up on the clutch and giving just the right amount of gas without spinning out. That day ended with our stalled car on a hill and a line of impatient motorists behind us, so we headed to a friend's car lot and borrowed one of his for practicing. Eventually, after trials and errors, they became great drivers, much better than I, even with a stick shift!

We operators in Holy Spirit's gifts are works in progress. We can't get ahead of ourselves, or catastrophes can happen. We should look for signs, slow down sometimes, and know progression comes by each experience as Holy Spirit and mentors help us hone our gifts. We should take what we've read, seen, or heard; make it real-world experience; listen to more seasoned operators; and cautiously proceed. But we'll never truly learn until we do it. We *will* get stronger, better, and more confident despite inevitable mistakes. We'll get to where it's so natural we wonder how anyone lives without it. Today, though, we're okay right where we are in our journey. I'm growing in Him still every day and couldn't navigate life's roads without His guidance. Your Arsenal of Holy Spirit? Those are Holy Spirit's gifts, and I can't imagine how I could survive without Him in the driver's seat.

Appendix

DREAMS AND VISIONS SYMBOLS
GLOSSARY

The following symbols have been compiled for many years from various sources, especially from the Bible and other dreamers who have shared their personal symbols.

Abdomen/ stomach	place of God's throne
Adder	false teachers
Adoption	ministry from someone else but is now ours, new convert (Rom. 8:15)
Airport	departing to new places, new idea or ministry taking off, [busy] desire for freedom, [empty] plans delayed
Alligator	someone talking (about us)
Almond	fruitfulness; resurrection (Num. 17:8)
Aloe	nature's fragrance, healing, relief
Altar	death, place of sacrifice and smoke
Amber	(see Gold)
Ambulance	first aid, pay attention to situation

Anchor	believers' security
Animals	(see individual animals) [babies] seemingly innocent things with potential for harm, [animal parts] inward parts of human nature
Ant	industrious, wisely prepares for future (Prov. 6:6-8), teamwork, unwanted guests, demonic attack
Apartment	(see House)
Apple	temptation, first fruits
Apple tree	(see Trees)
Ark	safety, salvation, place of glory and mercy
Arm	strength (Prov. 31:17), [outstretched] God's creative power (Jer. 27:5) or might (Exod. 6:6)
Armor	equipment for warfare, [armory] weapons storehouse
Arrow	God's Word, angels who move us forward, words, intercession (Zech. 9:14), something that pierces, suffering, conviction, prophetic words (2 Kings 13:15-19), God's judgment (Ps. 64:7), famine that destroys (Ezek. 5:16)
Asp	false teacher
Attic	past, memories, things put behind, things not used but might be in future
Axe	work instrument, judgment (Matt. 3:10)
Babies	new ministries
Babylon	evil system (Rev. 17:5)
Back	place to carry burdens, [hunchback] can't carry intercession's load or doesn't stand upright (Lev. 21:20)
Balance	weighs things of man, scarcity, stability

Balm	healing ministry
Banner	friendship, victory, standard lifted high
Barefoot	(see Feet)
Barley	Jesus (Passover harvest)
Barn	storehouse (Prov. 3:10)
Basement	below surface, unconscious mind, [messy] confusion to sort out or perceived shortcomings
Basket	provision
Bath	(see also Shower) thorough cleansing, [soaking] spending time in God's presence
Bathroom	place of cleansing from dirt or getting rid of waste
Beam	secure rafter of wood or iron
Bear (animal)	warning, [cub] something fierce appearing docile, evil, cunning, cruel, strong, ferocious men, God's judgment (2 Kings 2:23-24)
Beard	man's honor, [shaving another's beard] emasculation (2 Sam. 10:4-5), [clipped] mourning (Jer. 48:37)
Beasts	form of destruction (Jer. 15:3)
Beauty	holiness
Bed/Bedroom	place of spiritual rest
Bees/ Hornets/ Wasps	power to sting; host of people; biting words; affliction; produce sweetness; slander; persecution; trouble; offense; [swarming] demonic attacks (Deut. 1:44); [hornets] destructive trials (Deut. 7:20), God's tool for driving out enemy (Exod. 23:28), or fear and panic (Josh. 24:12)

Bell	tracks high priest's movement in Holy of Holies, victory in praise and worship, Holy Spirit's gifts (Exod. 39:26), sweet sound of God's voice
Belly	believers' spirits, where Holy Spirit dwells (John 7:38-39), place of compassion
Bicycle	small ministry, powered by much human effort
Binoculars	prophetically seeing, seems close but is not really
Bird	satan (Matt. 13:19), what could devour the Word (Matt. 13:4), something of little value to others but about which God cares (Matt. 6:26), form of destruction (Jer. 15:3), person receiving revelation about satanic snares (Prov. 1:17), [swallow] wanderer from nest, [blue] revelation coming
Bitter	[with sweet] God's Word which is sweet when you eat it but brings bitter judgment when you disobey (Rev. 10:9)
Black	God's absence, satan, liar, destroyer, evil, thief, sin, affliction, bondage, darkness, death, sorrow, famine, calamity
Black and white	victory, clear judgment
Blanket	spiritual covering
Blemishes	(spots) false teachers (2 Pet. 2:13), defect (Num. 19:2)
Blood	redemption, cleansing for sins (1 John 1:7), life, [above door] divine protection (Exod. 12:23), [sprinkling on garments] hallowed for God's service (Exod. 29:20), [bloody city] sheds innocent blood (Nah. 3:1), [poured under altar] martyrs' blood (Rev. 6:9-10), [with flesh] humanity (John 1:13), [dogs licking] death (1 Kings 21:19)

Blue	Holy Spirit, emotional lows, authority, God's presence, revealed God, divine revelation, faith, faithfulness
Body	dwelling for human spirit, tabernacle, God's temple (1 Cor. 6:19-20)
Bones	core of man (Ps. 6:2), [burn] commit atrocious action (Amos 2:1)
Book/ Scroll	[scroll] God's redemptive plan (Rev. 5:1), [of life] judgment (Rev. 20:12), [little] something that tastes good but is bitter to stomach (Rev. 10:10), [write in] preserve for future generations (Jer. 36:2), [destroy scroll] try to avoid or reject God's prophetic word (Jer. 36:23)
Boot	functional covering, works in many situations
Bottle	[wine] a person (Jer. 13:12)
Bow	[break] defeat in battle (Hos. 1:5), [treacherous] doesn't shoot straight (Hos. 7:16)
Bowl	[pouring out] God's judgment on man
Bramble	selfish, fruitless person
Branch	believer (John 15:5), church, Jesus (Isa. 11:1), [palm] rejoicing
Branch	(Olive—see Trees)
Brass	judgment against disobedience, what is refined (Rev. 1:15)
Bread	staff of life, Christ, our food, provision (John 6:32-35), [of mourners] unclean (Hos. 9:4)
Breast	balance of faith and love, place of love, ability to feed others spiritually, affection, intimacy, [beat] grieve (Luke 23:48)

Breastplate	righteousness (Eph. 6:14), judgment, protection of faith and love, covers heart for God (Exod. 28:30)
Breath	what makes man a living being (Gen. 2:7), Holy Spirit's infilling (John 20:22)
Briar	curse (Gen. 3:17-18)
Brick	human works (Exod. 5:7)
Brimstone	[with fire] God's judgment (Gen. 19:24)
Broad place	spaciousness or not hemmed in (Ps. 18:19)
Brocade	worn by kings
Bronze	God's judgment, fire of testing, strength
Brother/ Sister	Christians, those who do God's will (Matt. 12:48-50)
Brown	compassion, pastor, humanism, manmade, spiritual
Builder	Jesus (Matt. 16:18)
Burnt offering	surrender to God
Buses	larger ministries, people, churches
Bush	place from which God speaks (Exod. 3:4), [burning] son of man or receiving one's calling (Exod. 3:2)
Cake	[unturned] aspects of person are good but others not well developed (Hos. 7:8)
Cave	hiding place (Rev. 6:15)
Calamus	(see Spices)
Calf	prayers, praise, thanksgiving from our lips, idol (Exod. 32:4), [fat] prosperity (Mal. 4:2), [fatted] high degree of honor to bestow on guest (Luke 15:27), [cut in two] make covenant (Jer. 34:18)

Camel	burden bearer
Candle	Jesus, light of world
Cars	ministry
Cassia	(see Spices)
Cave	place of refuge from discouragement (1 Kings 19:9)
Cedar tree	(see Trees)
Cell phone	mobility, receptive to new information
Chaff	unnecessary, will be destroyed, wicked
Chain	bondage (Jer. 40:4), darkness
Chariot	place of God, vehicle for swift movement, prophetic anointing, angelic ministry (Ps. 68:17), salvation (Hab. 3:8), something mighty but not more than God
Cheeks	humility and obedience (Matt. 5:39), [red] embarrassment, [smiting on cheekbone] defeat of enemies (Ps. 3:7), [strike with rod] extreme insult (Mic. 5:1)
Children	something new, something already birthed, newly established ministry, immature Christians (1 John 2:13)
Cinnamon	(see Spices)
Cistern	manmade religion (Jer. 2:13)
City	life's circumstances, permanency, stability
Clay	pliable human (Jer. 18:4)
Closet	secret place of prayer

Clothes/ Garment/Robe/ Mantle/ Coat	calling; anointing; favor (Gen. 37:3); protection; concealing; reveals person's current state; moral or spiritual qualities (Matt. 22:11); Holy Spirit; outward attitudes; appearances; behavior; covering (1 Kings 19:13); brokenness (Job 1:20); authority (2 Kings 2:8); righteousness (Isa. 61:10); [tearing another's robe] removing from leadership (1 Sam. 15:27-28); [being torn by oneself] grief and humility (Ezra 9:3); [changing garments] repentant and change of heart (Gen. 35:2); [not taking clothes off] warfare (Neh. 4:23); [filthy] sin (Zech. 3:4); [white] purity and victory (Rev. 6:11); [made of coarse hair] prophetic (Zech. 13:4); [soft] one with an easy life (Matt. 11:8), [white robes] those who came through trials with robes washed in Jesus' blood (Rev. 7:13-14), [give away] pledge for debt (Amos 2:8), [shaking] completion without responsibility for a matter (Acts 18:6)
Cloud	God's Shekinah glory, host of people, good or evil, Holy Spirit, God's direction (Neh. 9:12), protection (Isa. 4:5), God's anger (Lam. 2:1), place Jesus sits (Rev. 14:14), surrounding Jesus when He left earth (Acts 1:9) and at His return (Rev. 1:7), [moving] God taking us higher or answers coming (1 Kings 18:44), [standing still] season to wait on God's direction (Exod. 40:37), [swift] God's judgment (Isa. 19:1), [morning] goes away quickly (Hos. 6:4), [without water] empty, doomed people who deceive others (Jude 12), [of smoke] signal of ambush (Judg. 20:38)
Cluster	group of believers

Coal	[of fire] judgment (Ezek. 10:2), [heaped on head] God's justice for enemies (Rom. 12:20)
Coat	(see Clothes)
Coffin/ Tomb	death; religious spirit; [whitewashed] someone looks good but is full of dead bones, uncleanness, hypocrisy (Matt. 23:27)
College classes	place of advanced preparation, [classes not attended] unprepared
Colors	(see individual colors)
Colors (bright)	favor, joy of the Lord
Colt	stubbornness, burden-bearer, avenue to bring Jesus into man's presence (Mark 11:7)
Concrete	hardness, solidity, walkway, obedience
Convention	need for communication to bring aspects together
Cord	[scarlet] hope or salvation (Josh. 2:18-19), Jesus
Corn	seed of healing, harvest, hope, God's word
Corner	place with no escape, [four] reaching everywhere, [sit in] place of discipline
Couch	rest, comfort, hospitality, lair, ambush
Courthouse	legalism
Cow	prosperity, wealth, produces mild foods and products, [fat] years of plenty or [gaunt] famine (Gen. 41:26-27), wife who's bad to others (Amos 4:1)
Crimson	(see Red)
Crops	time, season, harvest (Gen. 8:22)
Cross	Jesus' victory over death, faith, judgment

Crown	glory, righteousness, Jesus as king over heaven and earth, victory, priestly, ability to judge righteously, dominion, reigning, rewards (Rev. 4:4)
Crystal	Holy Spirit's cleansing, God's blessings, truth, clarity, sanctification, Bride of Christ, transparent, pure, renewed mind
Cup	fullness of joy, God's wrath due to sin (Isa. 51:17), [putting another's in your hand] receiving same judgment as another (Ezek. 23:31)
Curtains	temporary covering, keeps people from seeing private things
Cymbal	joy
Cypress tree	(see Trees)
Dad	God, heritage
Dance	victory over enemies, expression of joy and worship (1 Sam. 18:6-7)
Darkness	great tribulation, eternal state, ignorance, place of secrets to be revealed (Luke 12:3), demonic place (Jude 6)
Darts	enemy attacks
Dawn	Christ's return, revelation (2 Pet. 1:19)
Death	dying to self
Deer	panting for water of Word (Ps. 42:1), swiftness, agility, beauty, [fawn] inner quality of sensitive spirit
Diamond	enduring, great value, God's saints, [jasper] purity and holiness (Rev. 4:3)

Dog	friendly, demonic, unbelievers (Matt. 15:26), evil workers (Phil. 3:2), form of destruction (Jer. 15:3), [howling] dissatisfied (Ps. 59:14), [dog's head] contemptible thing (2 Sam. 3:8)
Donkey	lowliness; patience; strength; endurance; service; [wild] untamed human nature, stubborn, self-willed
Door	decision to be made, entering or leaving, Jesus (John 10:7), entrance to life, truth, beginning of Holy Spirit walk, [open] where satan may come into lives or godly opportunity (Rev. 3:8), [locking] closing satanic opening
Dove	Holy Spirit, gentleness, sacrifice, peace, [eyes] singleness of vision or spiritual insight, [turtle] Holy Spirit poured out through Jesus' sacrifice, [silly] someone easily misled (Hos. 7:11)
Dragon	serpent, [red] satan (Rev. 12:3)
Dream in a Dream	destiny, something God doesn't want us to miss
Dust/Soil	man (Gen. 2:7); inactivity or neglect; death or old flesh; frail human nature; satanic attack (Gen. 3:14); multitude of earthly seed; human heart; mourning (Lam. 2:10); [throwing into air or on head] sign of disgust, mourning, or disgrace (Acts 22:23); [shaking dust off feet] move forward from rejection (Matt. 10:14)
Dwarf	immaturity (Lev. 21:20)
Eagle	Spirit-filled believer (Isa. 40:31), strength, prophetic, swiftness of flight, realization of goals

Ear	way to receive faith, [pierced] those who choose to be His slave for life (Exod. 21:6), [stopped up] refusing to hear truth (Zech. 7:11), [blood on tip of right ear] hearing from God (Exod. 29:20), [speaking into] place of secrets (Luke 12:3), [incline] listen to (Isa. 55:3), [give an ear] listen (Joel 1:2)
East	mind of Christ, openness toward God
Eczema/ Scab	bitterness, unhealed wound (Lev. 21:20)
Elephant	wisdom, strength
Elevator/ Escalator	rising or lowering quickly, going to another level
Emerald	God's glory or saints
Eunuch	no fertility or reproduction (Lev. 21:20)
Eye	sight; insight; vision; eternity (Rev. 1:14); lamp of body (Luke 11:34); [blind or defective] deceived, no vision, or skewed vision (Lev. 21:18,20); [putting hands on] death (Gen. 46:4); [lifting] worship God or idols (Ezek. 33:25); [seven] complete knowledge and insight (Rev. 5:6); [put out right eye] bring reproach (1 Sam. 11:2); [flaming] omniscience, wisdom (Rev. 1:14); [to eye another] look at suspiciously (1 Sam. 18:9)
Eye salve	anointing, healing for eyes
Face	how we're recognized, [covering] showing humility and repentance (Gen. 32:20), [turning to wall] desperately going to God (2 Kings 20:2), [red/blushing] shame (Jer. 8:12), [falling on] reverencing God (Ezek. 3:23) or failing, [between knees] intense prayer or travail (1 Kings 18:42)

Faceless Female/ Male	angel, Holy Spirit
Fat	(from animal) inward part of offering, inward warmth, health, energy, prosperity
Feast	rich fellowship with God, abundance, celebration
Feathers	covering, protection (Ps. 91:4), flight, [chicken] annoyances
Feet/Barefoot	lowliness, walk, vulnerability, sensitivity to God, instrument of peace (Isa. 52:7), [barefoot] humility or slave in Master's presence, [broken or using crutches or walker] Christian walk not right (Lev. 21:19), [of clay] man's weak governments (Dan. 2:33), [washing another's] humility (John 13:6)
Field	world (Matt. 13:38), place of hidden treasures (Matt. 13:31), fertility
Figs	Israel, [good] those God will bless because of commitment to Him (Jer. 24:2,6), [bad] those who will be judged for refusing to commit to God, [placed on body] healing (2 Kings 20:7)
Fig tree	(see Trees)
Finger	little effort (Matt. 23:4), how God pronounces judgment (Dan. 5:24)
Fir tree	(see Trees)
Fire	purifies (Num. 31:23) or destroys (Exod. 13:21-22); Holy Spirit; protection (Zech. 2:5); prophetic word desiring to come forth (Jer. 20:9), God's Word (Jer. 23:29), invading armies (Ezek. 15:7), judgment (Dan. 7:11), trials (1 Pet. 4:12)

Fish	men, Christians, [clean or unclean] men's souls, [good] those saved (Matt. 13:48), [bad] those who reject God (Matt. 13:49)
Fishermen	angels (Matt. 13:49-50), disciples to lost
Flag	countries, worship, [white] surrender
Flame	(see Fire)
Flamingo/Stork	instrument to carry out God's purpose, baby's coming
Flax	man's weakness
Flock	God's people
Flour	crushing, refinement, healing tool (2 Kings 4:41)
Flower	fragrance of God, blooming of God's people, shortness of man's life (Job 14:1-2)
Fly	unclean, corrupt, demon, curse, nuisance, [dead] actions that cause shame to those who are respected (Eccles. 10:1)
Flying	future life in Holy Spirit, new perspective, high spiritual advancement
Food	spiritual sustenance
Forehead	mind, memory, thoughts, reason
Foundation	establishing cities, basics, buildings, churches, families
Fountain	Holy Spirit
Fowl	[unclean] evil spirits
Fox	burrower, cunning, evil men (Luke 13:32), suck lambs' blood, [little] small things which create problems (Song of Sol. 2:15)

Frog	evil spirits, uncleanness, [coming from mouth] appear to be great signs but are actually demonic (Rev. 16:13-14)
Fruit	life; how to determine one's character (Matt. 7:20); evidence of good land God's giving (Deut. 1:25); productivity; [pomegranate] Holy Spirit's fruit (Exod. 39:26), fruitful or joyful; seeds; godly thoughts
Fuchsia	(see Magenta)
Furnace	trials, affliction, judgment (Matt. 13:50), place of purification (Ps. 12:6), meant for destruction but where God shows Himself mighty (Dan. 3:25)
Furniture	personal preferences, can be functional or frivolous, [old] in need of restoration or one who's weathered time
Game	what one is playing or doing, immature activities
Garden	believer's soul, beauty of life in Jesus
Garlic	(see Leeks)
Garments	(see Clothes)
Gate	man's mind, new level in Christ (Neh. 3), [straight or narrow] righteous choices (Matt. 7:14), [rebuke at gate] judge another (Amos 5:10)
Gems	(see Jewels)
Gift	Holy Spirit's gifts (1 Cor. 12:4-11), talents
Goat	Christ, sin offering (Lev. 3:12-17), unredeemed sinner, those judged for sins of omission (Matt. 25:41,45), demon
Gold (metal)	divine nature, God, of great value

Gold/ Amber (color)	God, holy, hallowed, eternal deity, kingliness, glory of God's flaming throne, God's temple, wisdom, God's glory, Father's care, fiery passion, purity, trial by fire
Grain	sons of Kingdom (Matt. 13:38), [in sieve] God separating faithful from unfaithful (Amos 9:9)
Grape	fruit of vine, [eating sour grapes] committing sin (Ezek. 18:2)
Grass	man's withering glory, something temporary (Isa. 40:6-7)
Grasshopper/ Locust	small nuisance, man's assessment of his weakness (Num. 13:33), destructive enemies (Joel 2:25), evil spirits, something which torments (Rev. 9:3-5), [multitude] overwhelming troubles or destruction (Exod. 10:14)
Gray	spiritual warfare, mourning
Green	conscious, praise, charity, eternal life, healing, health, hope, spring, trinity, freshness, vigor, prosperity, flourishing
Gun	aggression, anger, potential danger, power to reach beyond yourself
Gymnasium	discipline, exercise
Hair	separation unto God, woman's glory, source of pride that could lead to downfall (2 Sam. 18:9)
Hallways	choices, different ministries, something leading somewhere
Hammer	God's Word (Jer. 23:29), crushing

Hand(s)	direction; Holy Spirit; will in action; fivefold ministry (1 Kings 18:44); service; something that could stand between you and God (Matt. 5:30); ministry; worship; strength; promise coming to fruition (1 Kings 18:44); exalts us after our humility (1 Pet. 5:6), destruction (Jer. 15:6), revelation (Ezek. 33:22); [broken] sin in our works (Lev. 21:19); [shake another's] make peace; [shake at another] judgment (Zech. 2:9); [right] fellowship, power, authority, protection (Rev. 5:1); [right raised] take oath (Dan. 12:7); [clean] righteousness (Ps. 18:20); [give into] be defeated by enemy as God's judgment (Jer. 34:20); [God's] provision, strength, makes whole (Job 5:17-18); [God's right] deliverance (Exod. 15:6); [cut] mourning (Jer. 48:37); [God's strong] power and might (Isa. 40:10); [washing] getting rid of personal responsibility (Matt. 27:24) or sin (James 4:8); [writing on] declaring you're God's (Isa. 44:5); [pouring water on another's] servanthood (2 Kings 3:11), [lean on] rely on as a helper (2 Kings 7:17)
Hare	unclean, satan and evil spirits
Harp	praise, worship, prophetic spirit
Harvest	end of age (Matt. 13:39), reaping what you've sown (Hos. 6:11)
Head	leadership, [lift up head] show favor to (Jer. 52:31), [shaving] sign of mourning (Ezek. 44:20), [of church] Jesus (Col. 1:18), [covering] ashamed and confounded (Jer. 14:3)
Headstone	memorial, repentance, death

Heart	love, man's condition with God (Jer. 17:5), deceitful and wicked (Jer. 17:9), man's character (Luke 6:45), [writing on] where God writes His law (Jer. 30:24), [cut to heart] conviction or anger (Acts 7:54)
Heel	crushing power, victory
Helmet	protection for mind, salvation (Eph. 6:17)
Hemlock	[in a field] destroys land's potential for fertility (Hos. 10:4)
Hen	one who gathers (Matt. 23:37), motherhood
Herb	food of earth, [bitter] suffering
High Rise	status, level of calling
Highway	holiness (Isa. 35:8)
Hips/ Thigh	strength, [exposed] faith, [putting hand under thigh] vow (Gen. 24:2), [Jesus touching hip] change of character (Gen. 32:25), [striking oneself on thigh] shame or humiliation (Isa. 47:2)
Hissing	shows contempt (Mic. 6:16)
Honey	sweetness of God's words (Ps. 119:103), His wisdom (Prov. 24:13-14), Holy Spirit, revelation and power (1 Sam. 14:27), [with milk] prosperity (Jer. 32:22)
Hornets	(see Bees)
Horns	seven Spirits of God (Rev. 5:6), nations (Zech. 1:21), power (Ps. 75:5), leaders or kings (Dan. 7:24), [seven] complete power, strength (Ezek. 29:21), [taller than others] stronger nations (Dan. 8:3), [holding horns of altar] protection (1 Kings 2:28)

Horse	good or bad, great power, purity, strength, warfare, swiftness, spiritual support, power of flesh, [red] brings war (Rev. 6:4), [black] brings economic lack (Rev. 6:5-6), [pale] brings disease and death (Rev. 6:8)
Hot air balloon	peaceful, rising in the Spirit
House/ Apartment	place of refuge; family, church, or job; dwelling; [unoccupied] neglect of secret place with God; [mother's house] grace; [birthplace] education or ministry roots
House- owner	disciple to lost (Matt. 13:51-52)
Idioms	(see end of Glossary)
Incense	saints' prayers (Rev. 5:8), [burning] worshiping idols (Jer. 44:8)
Ink	permanence (Jer. 36:18)
Iron or Irons	judgment against sin, inflexibility of rules, something unbreakable (Jer. 28:13), [mixed with clay] strong, but fragile (Dan. 2:42), bondage, [bound in irons] consequences of rebellion (Ps. 107:10-11)
Ivory	king's throne (1 Kings 10:18), temporary prosperity (Amos 3:15)
Jasper (also Diamonds)	God's glory
Jaw	[hook in] God drawing someone to Him (Ezek. 38:4)
Jewelry	[take off] show humility as God decides disobedience's punishment (Exod. 33:5)

Jewels/ Gems/ Stones	precious stones, church people, God's light or glory, glory of saints, words of wisdom and knowledge (Prov. 8:11), Christ, glory of Israel's tribes
Keys	authority over spirit realm (Matt. 16:19), [of David] Jesus (Isa. 22:22)
King	God (Matt. 22:2), Jesus
Kiss	intimacy, arm with weapons (1 Kings 19:18), greeting of love for Christian brothers (1 Pet. 5:14), betrayal (Matt. 26:48), [one's own hand] vanity (Job 31:27), [calf] worship idols (Hos. 13:2)
Knees	prayer (1 Kings 18:42)
Lamb	Jesus our sacrifice (Rev. 5:6), young believers, sacrifice for sin, meekness, offering, light (Rev. 21:23)
Lamp	wisdom, knowledge, God's Word, Holy Spirit, outward claim of following Jesus (Matt. 25:1), eye (Matt. 6:22), God's promise we can follow (2 Kings 8:19)
Lampstand	Holy Spirit, Lord (Zech. 4:11,14), church (Rev. 1:20)
Leaven	(see Yeast)
Leaves	self-made covering, [fading] time of God's wrath (Jer. 8:13)
Leeks/ Garlic/ Onions	food of world system, past we long for (Num. 11:5)
Legs	revealed word upon which believer stands, [lame] walk with God impeded or no walk with God (Lev. 21:18)

Leprosy	sin, living in corruption, backward living, destroys as it rots, unclean
Light	Christ and His church, Holy Spirit, eternal life, illumination or revelation (John 1:4), [under basket] covering gifts or talents (Matt. 5:15)
Lightning	God's anointed word going forth from believers
Lily	Bride of Christ, spiritual thoughts and words, [of Valley] Christ (Song of Sol. 2:1)
Limb (of body)	[won't work] something in spirit not fully or effectively operating, [too long] lack of balance (Lev. 21:18)
Linen	Jesus' purity, saints' righteousness (Rev. 19:8), worn by royalty or priests, holiness, sinless humanity
Lion	kingly authority, fearless, royal, ruler, strength, courage, boldness, good or evil men, nation (Hos. 5:13-14), [den] spiritual forces, [be cast in with] satan intending to destroy but God saves (Dan. 6:7), [roaring] devil (1 Pet. 5:8)
Lips/ Mouth	how we express our heart (Matt. 12:34), speech, snare (Prov. 6:2), [bridle in] being steered by God (2 Kings 19:28), [flattering] insincerity (Ps. 12:2), [in dust] submission (Lam. 3:29), [open mouth] speak badly against another (Lam. 3:46), [sacrifice of lips] repentance (Hos. 14:2), [uncircumcised] can't speak well (Exod. 6:30)
Locker	storage for personal items, put words in storage
Locust	(see Grasshopper)

Magenta/ Fuchsia	emotion, joy, passion, right relationship, compassion, heart of flesh
Man	God's image, intelligence, king of creation
Manna	God's provision (Exod. 16:14), divine food, life, health, sustenance but not plenty
Mantle	(see Clothes)
Mark	[on head] protection (Ezek. 9:4)
Mask	hypocrite
Meat	strong truth of God's Word for the mature, spiritual food, doing God's will
Merchant	seekers (Matt. 13:45)
Milk	elementary principles, truths of God's Word for sustaining the young (Heb. 5:13), Word that makes one grow (1 Pet. 2:2), [with honey] prosperity (Jer. 32:22)
Mire	filth of man's works, ungodly walk
Mirror	showing what we look like spiritually (2 Cor. 3:18), reflection, [broken] shattered self-image
Money	favor, loss of favor
Monkey	mocker, harasser
Moon	church purity, free from worldliness, [turned into blood] sign of Christ's return (Joel 2:31)
Mortar	fills gaps in wall, prophecies (Ezek. 22:28), [untempered] false prophecy (Ezek. 22:28)
Motel/ Hotel	transitional phase, secret meeting place
Moth	earth's destructive powers (Matt. 6:19)

Mother	those who do God's will (Matt. 12:48-50), one instilling values, foundation for godly walk, the nation (Hos. 4:5)
Mountain	God's Kingdom or world, problems, obstacles and trials (Zech. 4:7), the Law, something great that can experience devastation (Heb. 12:18)
Mouse/Rat	demons, feed off our lives' garbage, unclean
Mouth	(see Lips)
Mud	messy, sticky situations
Mule	stubbornness
Mustard	(see Seed)
Myrrh	(see Spices)
Nail	Christ, anti-Christ, sure (Isa. 22:23)
Naked	vulnerable, transparent, exposing oneself, shame (Hab. 2:15)
Names	Samples: [Deb] honey bee, era of leadership; [Connie] constant; [Alexander] protection of mankind; [Wade] place to ford stream; [Jacob] type of Jesus, supplanter
Neck	the will; [stiff] pride, arrogance, rebellion (Jer. 17:23); [under yoke] in servitude (Jer. 27:12); [placing foot on] defeat of enemy (Josh. 10:24)
Necklace	spiritual obedience adorning those who obey God's word (Prov. 1:8-9)
Nest	home (Hab. 2:9)
Net	power to catch souls, impending judgment at end of time (Matt. 13:47), invitation to lost, [spread] satan's snares (Prov. 1:17), [spread over someone] God's snare for judgment (Ezek. 17:20)

Noon	perfect light of day, sun's full strength
North	place of God's throne, God's judgment
Nose	discernment, sense of smell, [flat] no balance (Lev. 21:18), [hook in nose] steered by God (2 Kings 19:28)
Numbers	(see end of Glossary)
Oar	propels boat through water, prayer
Office	[building] work, administration, performance, function; [new office] new anointing
Oil	Holy Spirit anointing, readiness for Jesus' return (Matt. 25:4)
Ointment	unction, oil of the Spirit
Olive Tree/ Branch	(see Trees)
Onions	(see Leeks)
Orange (color)	perseverance, stubbornness, fire, fall harvest, healing, passion
Owl	night bird, evil spirit, demonic, wisdom
Oxen	people, human strength (Num. 23:22), servant's labor, Christ, sacrifice, burden-bearing, apostles, disciples, ministers to support (1 Tim. 5:18), God's servants, will subjected to God, [licking up grass] like God will lick enemies (Num. 22:4)
Palm tree	(see Trees)
Paneling	covering, something that beautifies outside but neglects God (Hag. 1:4)
Park	place of gathering, recreation, fellowship, common area
Pathway	[steep] call to rise higher in Christ

Peacock	ornamental, pride
Pearl	precious, truths, values, formation through suffering, Jesus (Matt. 13:45-46), church
Pierced ear	(see Ear)
Pig	unclean, messy situation, demonic, ignorance, hypocrisy, religious unbelievers
Pillar	overcomer (Rev. 3:12), solid Christian
Pink/Rose	Messiah, glory, Rose of Sharon, new life
Plague	judgment (Rev. 18:4)
Plane	large corporation, big ministry
Platter	lots of spiritual food coming, [silver] offering to God (Num. 7:13)
Plow	[putting hand to it] working for God (Luke 9:62), [looking back while plowing] not fit for Kingdom (Luke 9:62)
Plumb	line used to measure God's people (Amos 7:7-8), God's Word
Pome-granate	fruitful or joyful, Holy Spirit's fruit, seeds, godly thoughts
Pool	(see Water)
Porch	how we display ourselves, what others see but not what's inside
Potter	God (Jer. 18:4)
Present	(see Gift)
Prison	bondage, tests (Rev. 2:10)
Purple	kingship, kingly authority, majesty, nobility, power, royalty, wealth, inheritance
Purse	secrets held closely and guarded, finances, woman's intimacy, personal

Rabbit	reproduce quickly, multiply, destructive
Rain	revival, refreshing, outpoured Word and Spirit
Rainbow	God's covenant seal to earth and mankind, mercy (Gen. 9:12-13)
Rat	(see Mouse)
Raven	evil spirit, connected with famine, unexpected provision source (1 Kings 17:6)
Razor	sharpness
Reapers	angels (Matt. 13:39)
Red/ Crimson/ Scarlet	blood atonement, sacrifice, death, power, redemption, anointing, anger, war, cross, destruction, Jesus' blood, love, courage, martyr, sacrifice, sovereign power, wisdom, [scarlet clothes] valiant in battle (Nah. 2:3)
Reins	heart's motives, keeping in check
Remodeling	refreshing, renovation
Ring	adornment, [signet] divine calling and appointment (Hag. 2:23), [wedding] marriage and commitment to Jesus
Rise	[early] persistence to make others hear (Jer. 7:13)
River	God's blessings, move of God, Holy Spirit's flow, [stagnant] dead (Ezek. 47:11)
Roach	infestation, unclean spirits, uncleanness, hidden sin, dwells in darkness
Road	way to destiny, righteous choices (Matt. 7:14)
Robe	(see Clothes)

Rock/ Stone	solid, Jesus, support, stability, security, where God speaks face to face with man, [pillar of stone] judgment for disobedience (Gen. 19:26), [cut out without hands] symbol of God's power (Dan. 2:34), [cleft] secure place (Obad. 1:3)
Rod	authority to rule, measuring, judgment, God's wrath (Lam. 3:1), instrument of discipline (Prov. 13:24), [pass under] how shepherd counts sheep (Ezek. 20:37), [iron] weapon for destruction (Ps. 2:9)
Roller coaster	instability, emotional highs and lows
Roof	covering
Root	Christ, foundation, stability (Mark 4:17), goes deep, past issues you're holding on to, remnant assured for you (Dan. 4:26)
Rose (color)	(see Pink)
Rowing	human effort (John 6:19)
Ruby	Jesus' blood
Sacrifice	ransom, slaughter, reconciliation, redemption
Salt	enduring covenant, Christ's grace, saints' good or bad influence (Matt. 5:13), dead (Ezek. 47:11), purification (Ezek. 43:24), healing (2 Kings 2:21), [rub with] prevent growth of bacteria (Ezek. 16:4), [eating] sealing contract (Num. 18:19), [sowing on destroyed city] cursing with barrenness (Judg. 9:45)
Sand	earthly, natural, Abraham's seed, large number, unstable foundation on which to build (Matt. 7:26)
Sandals	(see Shoes)

Sapphire	anointing, God's revealed presence
Sash	pride (Jer. 13:7-9), clinging to God (Jer. 13:11)
Scab	(see Eczema)
Scales	justice, God's judgment for sin (Dan. 5:27), [deceitful] dishonest business practices (Hos. 12:7)
Scarlet	(see Red)
School	educational process, place to be with others of equal rank or pursuits
Scorpion	black magic, scourge, stinging whip, brings pain, demon (Rev. 9:3)
Scroll	(see Book)
Sea	upheaval; brings evil (Rev. 13:1); place hope arises (1 Kings 18:44); [glassy] God's presence (Rev. 4:6); [waves] humanity's restlessness, life's changing nature, trials (Mark 4:37)
Seed	Word (Mark 4:14); [good] Christians (Matt. 13:38); [mustard] purity, unrecognized potential (Matt. 13:31-32)
Serpent/ Snake	subtle, wise, deceptive, cunning (Gen. 3:1), sin, satan, lie, false story, God's judgment on rebellious people (Num. 21:6), [more than one] gossip
Shadow	[of God's wing] where He hides us from wicked (Ps. 17:8-9), [touching people] healing (Acts 5:15)
Shaking	removing things of earth so eternal may remain (Heb. 12:27)

Sheep	God's children, [ewes newly shorn] shedding issues, [wool or fleece] finding God's will (Judg. 6:37), [fat and strong] those who prospered at others' expense (Ezek. 34:16)
Sheer materials	freedom and lightness, joy in His presence
Shield	faith (Eph. 6:16), protection in battle, God (Ps. 3:3), [red] mighty men in battle (Nah. 2:3)
Ship	doctrine from Word, pass through water to carry what's useful, don't understand how sea supports (Prov. 30:19), something intrusive (Isa. 33:21)
Shoes/ Sandals	approach to life, diligence, Gospel of peace (Eph. 6:15), hard work, [old] convictions about beliefs or something comfortable, [removing one's sandal] giving up rights (Deut. 25:9), [exchanging] redeeming or confirming matter (Ruth 4:7), [removing on ground] standing on what's holy (Josh. 5:15)
Shoulder	place of strength, support, government (Isa. 9:6)
Shower	(see Bath) [taking one] cleaning up flesh, [rain] blessings (Ezek. 34:26)
Sickle	reaping of harvest, God's Word, reaping instrument (Rev. 14:15)
Side	[lying on] bearing nations' inequities (Ezek. 4:4)
Sieve	divine sifting
Silk	[humility] something precious created by something low, delicate
Silver	atonement, price of redemption, reconciliation, price of a soul
Sister	(see Brother)

Skirts	[lifting above face] public exposure and shame (Nah. 3:5)
Sleep	indifference, lack of diligence (Prov. 24:33-34), rest, death (John 11:11)
Slime	sin's mire
Smoke	Holy Spirit's power, worship, [smoke screen] deception (Rev. 9:2), [pillar] mark of God's presence or glory (Rev. 15:8)
Snake	(see Serpent)
Snow	God's glory, covers barren ground, fallowness, pure
Soap	cleansing from sin (Mal. 3:2)
Soil	(see Dust)
Sorcerer	drug dealer
Sparrow	has small value but important to God, of little note
Spices	anointing; costly; [cassia] useful for trading, used for intimacy, sweet-smelling; [myrrh] bitterness, healing from pain, connected with burial; [cinnamon] a place, world's fragrance, sweet-smelling; [calamus] used for sacrifice; [mint, anise, cumin] trivial things (Matt. 23:23)
Spider	sneaks into openings, activities and shrewdness of wicked, evil, sin, deception, false doctrine, occult
Spirit	[unfamiliar] not from God
Spoon	feeds young Christians
Spots	(see Blemishes)

Square	God's presence in ark of covenant (Holy of Holies), [New Jerusalem] the Church (Rev. 21:16)
Staff	shepherd's protection, [laying staff on face] discerning life in a situation (2 Kings 4:29)
Stairs	[higher or lower] going to another spiritual level
Star of David	Jesus, Israel
Stars	light bearer; Abraham's seed; Spirit-filled leaders; resurrection's glory; Israel; God's people (Dan. 8:10); light to dark world; angels (Rev. 1:20); authority and ruling (Num. 24:17); [morning] Jesus (Rev. 2:28); [fallen] apostates, anti-christ, demons
Stomach	(see Abdomen)
Stone	(see Rock)
Stones	(see Jewels or individual stones)
Stork	(see Flamingo)
Straw	withheld necessity (Exod. 5:7)
Stream	ministry
Stumble	disobey God's word (1 Pet. 2:8)
Stump	remnant assured for you (Dan. 4:26)
Sun	Jesus, God's glory, persecution or tribulation (Mark 4:6), light for world, scorching
Swallow	(see Bird)
Sweeping	new stance, fresh attitude, ignoring facts or intuition, [sweeping under carpet] covering up something, [house] getting rid of demonic presences (Luke 11:25)

Sword	God's Word (also coming forth from mouth) (Rev. 19:15), spiritual fight, powerful (Zech. 9:13), judgment (Hag. 2:22), form of destruction (Jer. 15:3), war (Jer. 29:18), [sharpening] impending judgment or instrument of judgment (Ps. 7:12, Jer. 9:16)
Tares	(see Weeds)
Tassels	holiness, reminder to obey God's commandments, healing (Mal. 4:2)
Tea	satisfaction of life, hospitality, comfort
Teeth	chewing on, biting things off, appropriating food, meditating on Word, [breaking ungodly's teeth] defeating enemy (Ps. 3:7), [broken] starvation, [clean] lack of bread (Amos 4:6), [baby teeth falling out] getting rid of childish things to prepare for more mature
Temples	(body) seats of man's thoughts (1 Cor. 3:16)
Tenants	religious people who don't accept Jesus (Matt. 21:33), those who don't have ownership in Holy Spirit
Tent	covering for pilgrims or strangers, flesh and blood body (2 Pet. 1:13)
Thief	satan (John 10:10), [in night] unpredictable event (2 Pet. 3:10)
Thigh	(see Hips)
Thorns	life's cares (Mark 4:7,19), deceitfulness of riches, desiring other things than we have, Jesus' sacrifice, cursed earth (Gen. 3:18), enemies (Judg. 2:3)
Throne	God's sovereignty

Thumb	[blood on right thumb] performing godly duties (Exod. 29:20), [missing] inability to wield weapon (Judg. 1:6)
Thunder	sign of impending power, [seven] God's voice (Rev. 10:3)
Toe	balance, movement, extreme limb, [big toe missing] inability for sure footing in battle (Judg. 1:6)
Tomb	(see Coffin)
Tongue	blessings or cursings, creates something permanent (Ps. 45:1), [on roof of mouth] mute (Ezek. 3:26)
Tornado	powerful force, change in atmosphere, [dark] beware, [light] God's will is happening
Tower	strength against enemies, safety (Ps. 61:3), God's name, protection
Train	large church, corporation, denomination, ministry
Treasure	Israel (Ps. 135:4), wisdom and knowledge, God (Ps. 73:25), Holy Spirit's power (2 Cor. 4:7), God's unique people (Eph. 2:10)
Trees	shelter, shade, people, beauty, oxygen, life, Christ, believers, sinners; [cypress] funeral tree, signifies death; [apple] Jesus in fullness of His love; [cedar] types of saints, righteous man's growth (Ps. 92:12), royal tree; [fig] Israel, blessing, [barren] Israel's barrenness; [fir] stately; [olive tree or branch] anointing, Israel (Rom. 11:17), church, peace, prosperity, people, beauty (Hos. 14:6), [dripping olive branch] anointed ones (Zech. 4:12,14); [palm tree] righteous man's flourishing (Ps. 92:12), upright, fruitful tree, oasis; [oak] solid, firm; [eating of] choices which affect destiny (Gen. 2:17)

Trumpet	warning (Rev. 8:6), prophetic voice, utterance, [silver] calling congregation and directing camp's movement (Num. 10:2)
Twins	double blessing, balance
Under-ground	something hidden
Under-water	Holy Spirit's deep things
Valley	trials, fertility
Vapor	life's fleeting quality
Vehicle	ministry, calling, gifting
Veil	hidden from world (2 Cor. 3:15-18), something which blinds minds (2 Cor. 3:14), façade we remove in God's presence (Exod. 34:34), modesty (Gen. 24:65), bride, separates us from God's presence (Exod. 40:21) [torn in two] entrance into God's presence (Luke 22:45)
Village	[unwalled] place
Vine	Christ and His church
Vineyard	Israel, God's Kingdom, church, bringing forth fruit, spiritual potential (Prov. 24:30), place Holy Spirit is nurtured
Violet (color)	love, passion, repentance, sorrow, suffering
Viper	evil deeds or spirits, satan, religious leaders or spirits
Voice	[still, small] Holy Spirit or revelation
Vomiting	purging
Vulture	unclean, evil spirits, demonic powers
Wading	beginning Holy Spirit walk

Walking	our own effort, how we advance
Wall	[whitewashed] hypocrisy, clean outside but bad inside (Acts 23:3)
Wallet	financial resources, self, holds personal identity, burden bearing
Wasps	(see Bees)
Water/ Pool	something to immerse in, life of peace and calm, Holy Spirit, humanity, God's Word, [clear] refreshing, [dirty] Holy Spirit perverted or neglected, [many waters] commanding authority (Rev. 1:15) or God's voice (Ezek. 43:2) or overwhelming troubles (Ps. 18:16), [sweet and bitter] need for Christian purity (James 3:11), nations (Rev. 17:15), purifying from sin (Num. 19:9)
Weeds/ Tares	sinners (Matt. 13:38), counterfeit, what denigrates
Well	Holy Spirit (Jer. 2:13), believer's spirit, salvation's waters, eternal life, [without water] false teachers with nothing to give (2 Pet. 2:17)
Wheat	source of bread, staff of life, souls to be harvested
Wheel	man's spirit (Ezek. 1:20)
White	God's or Holy Spirit's presence, Christ's Bride, Creator, holiness, innocence, saints, purity, righteousness, light
Wind	Holy Spirit, blows away what God purged, good or evil spiritual powers
Window	light, illumination, blessing of heaven, joy, Holy Spirit

Wine	new covenant, blessings, Christ's Bride, joy (Ps. 104:15), surrender, fellowship of Christ's suffering, drunkenness (Jer. 13:12-13), fragrant (Hos. 14:7), [new] Holy Spirit, a fruit of Holy Spirit
Wings	swiftness, wisdom, defense, strength, healing (Mal. 4:2), protection (Ps. 91:4), flight, God's Word, [take someone under wing] marry (Ruth 3:9)
Witness	Jesus (Rev. 1:5)
Wolf	satan, wicked or false teachers, destroys God's flock, subtle evil
Wood	mankind, carnality
Wool	makes one sweat (Lev. 19:19), man's effort, tends to gather dirt, [on sheep] needs regular shearing
Worm	despised, instrument of judgment, humility, Jesus, something that causes damage (Jon. 4:7)
Writing	[on wall] judgment (Dan. 5:25), [on front and back] can add nothing to what's already complete (Rev. 5:1)
Yard	extension of ministries
Yeast/ Leaven	faulty doctrine (Matt. 16:6), power that changes what it touches, penetrates lives, evil's corrupting power (1 Cor. 5:6-7), influences, what's hidden in heart, sin, hypocrisy
Yellow	mind, hope, fear, joy, celebration, light, glory revealed
Yoke	bondage (Jer. 27:8), [with Jesus] freedom
Zion	those who trust in God (Ps. 125:1)

Idioms

Idioms are expressions that are not to be taken literally. Often a dream's details will be presented as an idiom to give you direction. These are a few examples:

Barking up the wrong tree	made a wrong assumption
Biting off more than we can chew	not able to complete a task
Cart before the horse	getting things out of order
All our eggs in one basket	should diversify
Grass is greener on the other side	want what we can't have
Horse of a different color	it's a different issue
Piece of cake	really easy
Skeletons in the closet	things hidden
Handwriting on the wall	a matter is determined
We can lead a horse to water...	others have free will

Numbers

0	seed
1	unity, number of God
2	union, multiplication or division, witnessing, man's witness, matter determined by God
3	resurrection, Holy Spirit, fullness of God, Godhead, witness of God, divine perfection, completeness
3½	testing, fulfillment or length of drought (James 5:17), days before resurrection (Rev. 11:11)
4	completion of New Creation, God's creative work

5	God's grace, goodness, redemption, anointing, number of God's obedient people who can defeat 100 (Lev. 26:8), [months] length of trials (Rev. 9:10)
6	man's number and weakness, satan's evils, sacrifice to God (Ezek. 46:4)
7	completion (Rev. 15:1), man's spiritual perfection, abundance, (Mark 8:20), fullness, Holy Spirit, rest (Gen. 2:3), churches or angels (Rev. 1:20), [seals] nothing can be added (Rev. 5:1)
8	resurrection, new beginnings, new birth (Luke 2:21), teacher
9	matter's conclusion, finality, divine judgment, fruit and gifts of the Spirit, divine completeness, evangelist
10	fullness of testing, testimony, law, responsibility, journey, wilderness, nurture, pastor
11	judgment, disorder, transition, standing in gap, prophet
12	divine governmental perfection and order, apostle, Holy Spirit, abundance (Mark 8:19)
13	depravity, rebellion, apostasy
14	deliverance or salvation, double perfection and anointing
15	rest, reprieve, mercy
16	love, established, new beginnings
17	victory, God's elect
18	bondage, coming of age
19	faith
20	expectancy, redemption
21	exceeding sinfulness, pursuit of breakthrough (Dan. 10:13)

22	light
23	death
24	priesthood, worship (Rev. 4:10), the redeemed around God's throne (Rev. 4:4)
25	forgiveness of sins, begin ministry training
30	consecration, maturity for ministry (2 Sam. 5:4), Christ's blood, full stature, stepping into destiny (Gen. 41:46), [pieces of silver] price for betrayal (Matt. 27:3), [days] period of mourning (Num. 20:29)
35	hope
40	probation, testing (Matt. 4:2), closing in on victory or judgment (Num. 13:25), deliverance, testimony, completed rule, long time (Gen. 7:4), enlarged dominion (2 Sam. 5:4), days of enemy oppression (1 Sam. 17:16)
42/424	Israel's opposition, Christ's genealogy (Matt. 1)
50	getting back what satan stole (Jubilee), Holy Spirit's anointing, God's organization (Mark 6:40), liberty (Lev. 25:10)
60	pride
65	apostasy
70	universality, Israel, [days] answered prayer (Dan. 9:24), [times 7] infinity (Matt. 18:22)
72	combination of fruitfulness and perfection (Jewish tradition says number of gold bells and pomegranates on high priest's robe)
75	separation, cleansing, purification
77	unrestricted, unlimited fullness (Gen. 4:24)
100	God's election of grace, children of promise, God's organization (Mark 6:40), number of God's obedient people who can defeat 10,000 (Lev. 26:8)

120	divine period of probation, end of flesh
144	Spirit-guided life, overcomers
153	fruit bearing through Holy Spirit (John 21:11), Kingdom multiplication
200	brought by God's grace into place of deliverance, rest, enlarged dominion, insufficiency
300	divine deliverance, complete
400, 450	false prophets (1 Kings 18:19)
600	warfare
613	Jewish law (Jewish tradition says number of seeds in pomegranates and laws in Torah)
666	number of beast, Antichrist, lawlessness
1,000	God's glory, fullness, complete, period of reigning and subduing satan (Rev. 20:6)
1,335	true or false doctrine, influence, end of trials (Dan. 12:12)
3,000	insufficiency without God (1 Sam. 13:5), God's judgment (Exod. 32:28)
7,000	remnant working for God (1 Kings 19:18), complete but limited group (Rev. 11:13)
10,000	seed in God's image through testing, ultimate (Ps. 91:7), great number (Rev. 5:11), [times 10,000] innumerable (Rev. 5:11)
72,000	[12 legions times 6,000] way of escape (Matt. 26:53)
144,000	remnant of Israel who remained pure (Rev. 14:1)

NOTES

Revelation Gifts

1. Graham Cooke, *A Divine Confrontation* (Shippensburg, PA: Destiny Image, 1991), 192.

2. James Strong, *New Strong's Exhaustive Concordance* (Nashville, TN: Thomas Nelson Publishers), G154.

3. Strong, G2212.

4. Strong, G2925.

Words of Knowledge

1. Strong, G1108.

Unctions

1. Strong, H1827.

2. Jack Hayford, *New Spirit Filled Life Bible* (Nashville, TN: Thomas Nelson Bibles, 2002), 471 center note.

3. Strong, G5545.

4. Strong, G1097.

5. Strong, H5916.

Visions

1. Strong, H2374.
2. Strong, H2377.
3. Neal Snyder, "July 12, 2012—SnyderTalk Editorial: The Wilderness Journey Comes to an End," *Snyder Talk,* July 11, 2012, http://www. snydertalk.com/?p=23673.
4. Strong, G3706.
5. Strong, H2384.
6. Strong, G3701.
7. Strong, G3705.
8. Strong, H4758, from H7200.
9. Strong, G1611, from G1839.

Words of Wisdom

1. Strong, G4678.

Dreams

1. Hayford, "The Book of Genesis," 54, "Kingdom Dynamics" note.
2. Ibid.

Tongues, Interpretation, and Praying in Holy Spirit

1. Hayford, "The Book of Isaiah," 870 introductory notes; "The Acts," 1485 introductory notes.

Prophecy

1. Strong, H2371, from H2372.

Faith

1. Strong, G4690.

Gifts of Healing

1. Strong, H5401.
2. Ask.com, "How Long Can Humans Last Without Water?" Mega Filter Network, Inc. June 29, 2006, http://ask.metafilter.com/41162/how-long-can-humans-last-without-water.
3. Strong, G3875.
4. Hayford, "Word Wealth," 1470.
5. Strong, G2323.

Harnessing His Power

1. Strong, G1849.
2. Strong, G1410.
3. Strong, G1412.
4. Strong, G1414.
5. Strong, G1415.
6. Strong, G1411.
7. Strong, G680.

Intercession

1. Strong, H6293.
2. *Holy Bible*, "KJV Interpreting Dictionary," (Gordonsville, TN: Dugan Publishers, Inc.), 1.
3. Ibid.
4. Ibid., 5.

5. Ibid., 8.

6. Ibid., 5.

7. Ibid., 3.

8. Strong, G2540.

9. Strong, G1982.

10. Strong, G3341.

11. Strong, G1793.

WADE AND CONNIE HUNTER-URBAN

Wade was raised on a farm in Franklin County, Indiana, by Christian parents. He was active in sports through high school and received an appointment to the United States Military Academy at West Point, New York. Wade graduated with a B.S. in Engineering and was commissioned an infantry officer in the U.S. Army. He served various assignments, including Vietnam where he was three times decorated for valor in combat. Connie was born in Oxford, Ohio. She earned a B.S. in English and an M.A. in secondary education from Miami University. She taught high school for 33 years before retiring.

Connie and Wade long to be about the Father's business. They're founders of Restoration Ministries, a blacksmith ministry to help others hone their Holy Spirit tools. They minister together as Kingdom equippers, helping believers discover and grow in the gifts of Holy Spirit. They speak at conferences and churches, conduct workshops, host services, blog frequently, publish a ministry newsletter, write books, and stream live from their home each week with teaching and intercessory prayer. They minister with frequent words of knowledge and prophecy, with many miracles occurring in their services. Connie has three published books, *God's Plan for Our Success Nehemiah's Way*, *The Elijah Anointing*, and a children's book, *Butchie Finds a Home*. *Your Holy Spirit Arsenal* is the Urbans' first co-authored a book.

Contact info:
Wade and Connie Hunter-Urban
P. O. Box 634
Connersville, IN 47331
Phone: 765-825-2030

OTHER BOOKS BY
CONNIE HUNTER-URBAN

*Your Holy Spirit Arsenal: Waging Victorious Warfare
Through the Gifts of the Spirit*
(Co-authored with Wade)

The Elijah Anointing: Empowering the Prophetic Gift

*God's Plan for Our Success Nehemiah's Way:
Rebuilding the Gates in Your Christian Journey*

The Josie Adventures: Butchie Finds a Home

FREE E-BOOKS?
YES, PLEASE!

Get **FREE** and deeply discounted **Christian books** for your **e-reader** delivered to your inbox **every week!**

IT'S SIMPLE!

VISIT lovetoreadclub.com

SUBSCRIBE by entering your email address

RECEIVE free and discounted e-book offers and inspiring articles delivered to your inbox every week!

Unsubscribe at any time.

SUBSCRIBE NOW!

LOVE TO READ CLUB

visit **LOVETOREADCLUB.COM** ▶